The Secret Life of

TINDERfella

The funny side of what he's thinking

Peter Benn

Argosy Media

PETER BENN

All contents copyright © Peter Benn 2018

All rights reserved worldwide under the Berne Convention.

First published: United States of America 2018

Except for brief passages quoted in newspaper, magazine, radio, television or online reviews, no part of this book may be reproduced or transmitted in any form, by any means (electronic, photocopy, recording or otherwise) without the prior written permission of the publisher. Any trademarks, product names or business names are assumed to be the property of the respective owners and are used only for reference. There is no implied endorsement. All stories, including but not limited to, people, places, and content are fictitious.

As this is not a medical book, any activity, advice and/or information described is purely for adult entertaining storytelling purposes, is general in nature and non-specific to any individual, couple or group. It is not a substitute for your own common sense. You are encouraged to seek your own independent medical, psychological and counseling services. The author and publisher shall not be responsible for any person(s) with regard to any loss or damage caused directly or indirectly by the information in this book nor for any damages resulting from the misinterpretation of this work.

ISBN: 978-0-9954234-2-8

Published by Argosy Media
PO Box 7615, MELBOURNE, Victoria 3004 Australia
Email: info@peterbenn.com
Author Website: www.peterbenn.com

NINE INCHES OF PURE PLEASURE: AN INTRODUCTION 7
1. TEEN EXPERIMENTATION and FIRST SEX 15
2. MANSCAPING 39
3. JASON'S MANZILIAN 57
4. EUROPEAN VACATION 69
5. THE DEVIANT AND SINNERS SWINGERS GROUP 101
6. THE BRIDESMAID 125
7. THE CUM COOKBOOK 139
8. THE DREADED ZIPPER INCIDENT 155
9. THE ARCTIC BEARS 163
10. THE NIGHT OF THE NIPPLE RING 175
11. THE MISTRESS 187
12. NUDE BEACH 205
13. THE BI-CURIOUS TRACK JOCK 223
14. THE FLUFFER 247
POSTSCRIPT 259

Other Books by Peter Benn 263

PETER BENN

Over an autopsy, two female pathologists were discussing the theory of why men seemingly only think with their dick.

"Here's his little brain," said one.

"And here's his big dick," smiled the other.

Theory proved!

PETER BENN

TINDERfella

NINE INCHES OF PURE PLEASURE: AN INTRODUCTION

I am Jason Jackson's penis - his schlong, his wiener, his dick, cock, prick, his tackle – or whatever you would like to call me. I'm not embarrassed by The Dicktator, One-Eyed Snake, Rumpleforeskin (though I am cut) or Cock-a-Saurus Rex.

Nor human names like Willy, Roger or Vlad. Even John Thomas I'll answer to.

For the last twenty of his thirty-two years, I've been beaten, massaged, licked, sucked, bruised, poked and man and woman-handled into the most amazing of human orifices, and in the most diverse locations.

If you take an average of three dates a week where I ejaculate twice at each event, then in my twenty years of active sexual service I've already accounted for some 6,240 juice extractions. Add to that the far too-many-to-count additional masturbation moments (well, let's take a wild guess – once a day, every day x 20 years – Mmmm, I think that we can safely say around an additional 7,000 outpourings). So, you can see that with over 13,000 ejaculations notched into Jason's imaginary belt, PLUS all the multiple daily water-works activities, I have had very little time to just hang around shooting the breeze.

I've got two good friends, "The Balls" as I call them, as my partners in crime. They're connected to The Sperm Factory or Headquarters as I sometimes refer to it, where production schedules continually push out an over-supply of man-juice. Naturally "over-supply" means The Boss (Jason) must continually find new and frequent means of emptying these tanks, whether by hand or by insertion methods. Either way, it means that I'm directly involved.

Over the years I've rarely been laughed at as, with my nine plus inches (or 23cms) of length PLUS my thick girth, I can hold my head up high in any naked male company.

You can well imagine that by being attached to such a horny young man that I've observed and frequently been part of, the most interesting sexual debauchery and fun. And as you will discover, that's a true statement.

But I've also been ignored!!! The romance writers simply refer to me as his member, his privates or his manhood and the erotic writers are no better with organ, joystick, phallus or boner.

Hence it's time for me to tell MY side of the story. Welcome to my world - the late nights, the all-nights, the limp times, the stellar times, the ignored times. The itch, the sweaty jocks, the smelly urinals, the teeth - oh, yes

THE TEETH – the infections, the sunburn, the tight condom "raincoats", the public displays... and where Jason takes all the credit for sexual performance when in reality that credit belongs to me.

Some would say that like many men, he only thinks with his dick – and in a backhanded complimentary way, they are right. I'm always there, front and center, at ALL his sexual encounters – and without MY ever-reliable enthusiastic prowess, he'd be scoring a lot less often.

So, let's share some of the highlight moments of the last twenty years and see the world from my point of view.

And just a warning - it's a tell-all story that is so much fun that it could curl your pubes. And if you shave "Down There", then we'll come to that story too, along with the drama of waxing - and you know already how men l-o-v-e being waxed!!!!!!

Also, share with me the intimate world of pleasuring in the hands and bedrooms of the dominatrix, the porn star, the prostitute, the air hostess, the bridesmaid and the swingers group - to name but a few. And not forgetting that awkward once off, so-called "bi-curious" encounter with the handsome track jock while also remembering how it all began with those innocuous, early puberty "wet dreams".

Let's begin....

PETER BENN

But First, A Quick Word – A Disclaimer - from The Boss, my owner, operator and the so-called Brain's Trust in this body we share.

(Just between you and me, Jason really, really, REALLY insisted on this – of course, it's all reflective of his ego and his deluded self-image of being totally irresistible to women, you know. As we shall see, without me and my erectile reliability, it's all just willy-waving with no chance of a happy ending.)

"Irrespective of whatever Jason Junior "Down There" has told you - or will tell you, he is my Best Friend.

With my hand on his shaft, he leads me into the most amazing sexual adventures.

He always has my back, is my ever-trusty wingman and never leaves me to go off and do his own thing with someone else. He's true and loyal, hard-working for a medium-to-large size guy, likes to show off his head, loves getting and staying hard, reliably empties himself on demand, likes being clean and healthy, always hangs out a few inches ahead of me, always has one eye alert for new adventures for the two of us.

He doesn't mind wearing a "latex shower cap" when we're required to have safe fun (though we've both objected to those flavored "connies" (condoms or perhaps known as rubbers to you), especially the strawberry scented variety. How embarrassing it is to smell like a hot fruit salad at a juice bar when you're intensely concentrating on moving toward a climax with a delightfully perfumed young lady).

And what about his occasional "could do better" attitude?

Unfortunately, he doesn't seem to be able to cope very

well when I've had a few too many beers. He has been known to feign "brewer's droop" at the most inopportune time – generally without warning, very early in the morning in the bed of a total stranger. That's not a pretty sight for either of us.

And he can be lazy. I notice that he likes to take long rests curled up amidst my pubic hairs in a snug position in my tight jocks or alternatively, stretched out, dressed to the left, under my boxers just happily dangling like a dead doodle along my thigh.

He's had years of intensive training with one of the top professionals in M/F sexuality, that is, namely me - and together we now understand each other so well that one can lead the other without the other even being initially aware. Of course, we are both needed there together at the business end of the encounter but how we get there is the true adventure.

He's been there with me from Day One when I had my over-hanging fleshy wrapping cut off within hours of my birth (fortunately neither of us remember that little moment of un-anaesthetized surgery). Then there were the infections, the sunburn, the tough hymens, the anal probes, the zipper incident – oh boy, you name it, we've been there and done it, brothers in arms, together, inseparable, even in the face of tangled fiery-red pubes, freezing cold ocean water and wet dreams that seemed unlikely to ever end.

He's my bro, my buddy, my Best Friend, and this is HIS story, from HIS unique point of view (one-eyed though that might be) of some of the sexual fun he and I have had together over the last two decades.

Enjoy!"

*"Roses are red,
Violets are blue,
I'm using my hand
But I'm thinking of you."*

PETER BENN

CHAPTER ONE

TEEN EXPERIMENTATION and FIRST SEX

I've never been busier nor more in need of sleep than when Jason was a teen.

Up to around his thirteenth birthday, I was merely a curiosity, an appendage of no worth nor curiosity. I was noticed during toilet-training, laughed at and prodded by curious fingers of other children a few times during the intervening years, served my urinary purposes as best I could - and generally just hung around waiting for the wake-up call I knew I'd receive around that specific birthday time. A few sporadic hairs sprouted in his pubic region as a hint of things to come but there was little interest in me when compared to playing sports, riding bikes with his friends or asking the girls to show him their "tits". He was a total sexual innocent and had no idea what was to come and how his life was totally going to change. Later, when I became a full partner with him, I took the place of these other interests and became his new best friend, inseparable buddies, always in search of a new sexual adventure. And when there were no others to play with (and that was the usual state of affairs for the first couple of years of his growth spurt), we made our own fun together or occasionally with one other "curious" boy or girl.

One night during his twelfth summer, boy Jason was sleeping face down across the sheets having one of those fitful nights of restless sleep. I was under him, squashed firmly into the mattress as so often was the case. I could tell that he was having dreams, as he sometimes ground me even deeper into the mattress. Probably having dreams that connected to that instinctual urge to embrace puberty. Whatever he was dreaming about was sending me a message to grow hard to my full length. There had been a few times earlier where messages had gotten me into a semi-erection but by the time Jason had woken I'd long lost maintaining the urge and had limply slept on until he awoke oblivious to the night's activities.

But this night was different. As a result of his dreams I expanded to my full twelve-year-nearly-thirteen-year old capacity - admittedly not big as yet, but by comparison to what I'd seen in the school showers, I was doing more than ok. Jason would be happy with me when he finally got to see what I could do and what pleasures he could avail himself of by playing with me.

I was extended to my full length under him. He began to ride me as if slipping and sliding around on a waterslide. This naturally felt really good for me, having my whole shaft massaged up and down like that. The still hairless Balls also wanted to get in on the action so we all went along for the ride. Like me, they'd been just dangling around listlessly for years so they weren't familiar with all this pressure and attention. The movement very quickly got them excited too.

Simultaneously, coming down from the previously inactive Sperm Factory were messages that production had at last been quietly activated and that there was currently an overstocked supply of boy juice that needed to be released via the flood control muscles. Were The Balls and I in a position to combine together and allow this initial flow to happen unimpeded?

We telegraphed back that we were.

While these discussions were underway, Jason turned over onto his back leaving his stomach, and "Down There" naked to the world.

Well, guys, you know that feeling when sometimes your balls take control of you and when they want to empty there's no denying the little blighters their escape route. Such was the case in point. When Jason accidentally knocked his hand on to me as he turned over, the surprise of that on to my erection involuntarily released my long constrained ejaculatory muscles. With the pressures from The Balls pushing against my shaft, there was nothing else for it. Jason's first wet dream was pumped all over his chest, stomach, and stubbled pubes.

"It was a bit watery, had some white glug in it, and a blood spot" he voraciously told his avidly listening friends. "Warm when I first felt it pumping out, but then went icky cold and sticky. Not so nice. Had to wipe up with some facial tissues which my Mum found later crumpled up beside the bed and asked whether I was going down with a cold?"

"No Mum, just wiping up a wet dream" I wanted to say -

but couldn't." Instead, all I could mumble half-truthfully was "I'll get over it. It's just a passing virus..."

"Did it feel good?" a girl asked.

"Sure did. Can't wait to get to bed tonight to see if it will happen again."

"Can I have one too?" she plaintively asked, though realizing that she was missing just one vital, dangling appendage that the boys all seemed to have to play with.

"Nah - wet dreams are for boys, periods are for girls."

As the word spread around the school about my prowess in producing a good time for Jason while he slept, so he learned from the more experienced boys, that if you took hold of your dick and pumped up and down like a bicycle pump then, when it felt R-E-A-L-L-Y good, the slit would shoot out it's warm sticky contents for you.

With his friends Alec and Tim, I was then subjected to considerable pain and embarrassment as they tried to put into practice what the more learned boys had told them. Let me say right here and now - I AM NOT A BICYCLE PUMP!!! Speak of me in terms of sausage and I will accept the description, but not - I repeat - not a mechanical device for inflating tires. Yes, I appreciate that they were inexperienced boys, trying to be grown up and adult about what they had been told. I accept that thirteen-year-old boys have a strength they don't always appreciate that they have. But combine experimentation with over-eagerness and you have the recipe for what could only be described as excruciatingly painful "Wanger Rash". Six strong eager teen hands all attempting to twist me their way and not the direction of the others - WITHOUT LUBRICATION - is what I'd describe as extreme sexual torture.

Yow. Cringe. FAAAAAAARRRKKKK!!!! is how I remember it. It hurt like fury and when I was reduced to a limp tender mess there was no sympathy for why there was no longer an erection.

Just an admonishment that "You can't wet dream during the day without a stiffy" Tim reminded them. "Here, let me have another go" and reached forward to grab me again.

"Piss off" Jason cried out, acutely feeling my pain. "Leave him alone!"

If I hadn't been in so much pain I would have smiled inwardly to myself. It was the first, albeit un-thought-out acknowledgment that I existed in Jason's world. I was a "him", I was his pride and joy, I was now a vital part of his sexual future. From that day onwards I was no longer ignored. We were best friends. He soon learned that I was that vital instrument that existed between his female friend and himself, the difference between achieving pleasure and suffering lost possibilities, and enjoying the best fun that two friends could possibly have together. As was my creed: Ignore me and I'll retaliate with flaccid indifference; treat me as an equal partner and the world of all things sexual could be his for a lifetime.

"You need to stop masturbating so vigorously," said the doctor to Jason, as he held me limply but gently. "A friction burn like this on your penis isn't necessary. Use a bit of commercial drugstore lubrication if you can. Even your Mum's cold cream or her cooking shortening can be useful in an emergency."

Jason's Dad didn't know which way to look, for it was obvious that he fully appreciated from his own experiences the wisdom and knowledge that the doctor was imparting to his son. That meaty weapon he could see in the doctor's hands was like "a chip off the old block". He knew how important his own large appendage had been for winning the girls to his bed so it would be the same for young Jason.

He was also thinking that it was now high time for a more detailed "chat" with his son, a somewhat more practical one than just the theory of birds, bees, and babies. It was time for the lube, condoms, oral and hygiene one, as well as the-don't-get-her-pregnant one.

I couldn't have agreed more!

Dad's "chat" happened in the car on the way home from the medical facility. There was just the two of them and I was snuggly wrapped inside the warm jocks so that no additional chaffing would make me more tender than what I already was. The soothing cream with the mild anesthetic ingredient in it did give me a rather unusual sensation as if I was conscious but with very little feeling. When Jason eventually experimented with hallucinogens I think he had the same feelings as I did that night. Lots of "whoo-hoo wooing" and telling everyone how beautiful they were with their two heads.

As you could say, I was off with the pixies and in a weird drug-induced world of my own.

Hence everything I heard of "THE Conversation" remains a bit of a blur, but there were the awkward bits that have stayed in my memory...

Jason - "What! You put your Mum's cooking shortening

on your dick - and on the dick of your school friend too."

Dad - "We were young and experimenting - my older brother told me about these things... We were poor, so there was no money for proper store-bought lubrication. Yes, my friend Jack used to have sleepovers at my place. And we'd play with each other's dicks. It's just what curious kids did in those days."

Jason - "And what if I haven't got a condom with me when the girl says yes to sex?"

Dad - "Try to always carry one as you don't want to get her pregnant. Of course, if she's serious, she might have one in her bag. Or use cling wrap if it's a real emergency. Or pull out before you cum - though that isn't always successful," he added with a dejected voice that implied secret knowledge of an experience that was best left forever buried.

"Let's stop off here and get you a supply of proper lubricant and condoms, though I guess you won't need them for a while yet. Keep the lube tube under the bed next to the dirty magazines and your Mother will be alright with that. She'll understand and not ask questions. She had brothers too, you know. And when the lube runs out I'll slip you some extra pocket money to go buy some more. Just let me know."

Jason - "Thanks, Dad. I guess there are some things we guys just can't talk to Mum about. By the way, how many times a day can I shoot a load without hurting myself?"

Dad - "You'll know. It's when your balls start to ache. When I was your age, three seemed to be a good average for me - not counting the wet dreams of course. Or the accidents when Valmai Thurston would tease me with her cleavage."

I suspect that Dad already had a hint that his son was going to take after him - horny the whole time and always open to anything sexual.

But I did under-estimate the enthusiasm that young Jason showed for experimentation with me. WOW - did I ever underestimate him! It didn't help that one of his friends told him the more you exercised a muscle the bigger and stronger it became. Now, that might very well be the case for a torso or an upper arm, but it doesn't mean that I was similar. Jason began multiple 24/7 workout regimes for me, determined for me to grow in stature to the size of the biggest penis he had seen in the porn magazines that were stashed under his bed. If those men could please women with their nine-plus inches and mighty girth, then that's exactly what he wanted from me. And so, the masturbation exercise marathons began...

When waking up, under the shower, showing off in the school bathroom, between classes, under the sports showers, in the park on his way home, with his mates in their bedroom, under the house, in the garden shed, by the creek – it happened anywhere where his hand could slip under his shorts. It also included in front of his television, while reading the porn magazines, while voyeuring on the neighbor's wife, at the movies, on the late night walk home - you name it and I was on show quicker than a snake slithering on a frozen lake.

Whip me out, wank me, wipe me - it became so constant that I barely had time to recover before the next exhibition was upon me. The guys in The Sperm Factory were on a constant twenty-four-hour production schedule producing the white stuff almost as quickly as it got expelled. My outer skin did show signs of grazing and harsh abuse, so occasionally I had the pleasure of the cool soothing lube which was a blessed relief from the normally rough hands abusing me.

The girls swim team also didn't help my situation one little bit. With their increasingly abundant cleavage, their body-hugging swimwear and their pubescent body growth, my Jason became an ardent one-boy fan club. His imagination as to what was hiding under the swimsuits and what could be done with that knowledge invariably sent him into immediate rampant horniness – his brain constantly bombarding me with erection messages. Those Hormone Guys were just as bad, always trying to pressure me to perform way beyond my developing capacity generally allowed. It was like a vicious migraine headache the way they wouldn't take "no" for an answer. Push, push, push. They wanted abusive control over me.

"Come on, come on. Jason wants an erection" they would shout at me with all the bullying tactics they could muster. "He's seen Pattie's nipple shape pushing through her thin swimwear and now he needs to beat off".

Pattie Lefrage was a girl somewhat ahead of her class friends in regard to her feminine development. She was taller, bustier, more beautiful than they were, plus, she had a much older brother who had coached her in her dealings with boys. She, therefore, knew how to tease them and keep them interested, but according to the gossip, she also knew how to make a boy happy in bed. Remember, that this was the second half of the nineties where the internet and smartphones and sexting and live sex porn sites were still fairly much in the future, so back then the news was spread via the verbal grapevine as to who was doing what to whom and when. And the local grapevine was always hot with stories about Pattie and her conquests.

Jason heard the stories, saw the happy faces of those boys who had made a "favorable impression" on Pattie and he let his imagination run riot as to what it must be like to be alone with her - naked!

I was the used and abused part of that scenario. If Pattie was within sight of us, then there was no rest for me. As soon as practical, his hand was upon me and I was soon coughing up inside his jocks, on to the ground, inside his sock or wherever was convenient. I simply hated this girl and I hadn't even met her head-to-face let alone head-to-gash as yet. But that was to change during the summer vacation.

Jason guessed that the sports store was the best location to "accidentally" meet up with Pattie. He had long imagined the many scenarios that could play out for him to have his first ever sex with a girl, and Pattie was the one that he hoped it would be with. Mind you, any girl would have done, he just wanted to have the experience so that he could share it with his mates and therefore be accepted into the group as an adult rather than a wannabe. Sex was a rite-of-passage and he was determined that over this summer vacation he was going to lose his virginity one way or another. He'd even taken a bet with two male friends as to who would be the first to put their pleasure rod into a willing honey pot.

Pattie's "speed bumps", the name the boys admiringly referred to her breasts as, were now large and plump and so decidedly provocative that she always had a string of attentive guys around her. The word was also out that she actually had shaved her pubes "to make herself faster in the water". This latest piece of boy erection fodder continued to fan the flames of horniness so that the fires in the boys were now more like forest-fires. Jason knew he had steep competition in order to win her over, but in the sports store that morning he felt nothing less than confident.

And there she was - in the swimwear department emerging from the fitting room in a very revealing bikini. Unfortunately, I couldn't see anything from inside his shorts where I was having a free-balling day. Jason knew that I would show him up to best advantage without having the constrictions of a jock pouch to hold back his emerging mound. It was all part of the ploy to let Pattie admire and imagine what happiness Jason had waiting in his shorts for her to enjoy.

After several minutes of watching from the nearby racks of clothing, Jason moved towards her, me being in a semi-state, pointing the direction forward.

"Hi Pattie," a lay-back Jason said. "How's it goin'?"

"Do you like it?" she enquired of her new admirer. "It's the very latest for summer."

"Why yes - it shows your breasts off beautifully" he quickly replied. As soon as he said it, he instinctively knew it was wrong. It was his hormones doing the responding.

"Well, big boy, I thought so too" she replied with a wide smile. "Come with me and I'll show you the other choices" - and walked off into the fitting room area with her second finger indicating that she should be followed.

Like a lamb to the slaughter, he followed. The salespeople were busy with other customers so the two were alone in the cubicle.

The fitting room was exactly that - a series of individual rooms with full-length doors that could be locked from the inside. Pattie went in and Jason and I followed.

Jason's heart was pounding, his eyes and body alert to the potential danger of being caught in such a compromising situation.

Her hand was warm and pliable as she massaged me through Jason's shorts.

"Mmmmm I'd heard stories about you and your big friend... "Down There"..." she whispered to him. "And I now feel that it's all true...."

Down came the shorts and before I could appreciate the isolation of the cubicle, my now full erection was engulfed in darkness and warm saliva. The jolt that shot down to me from the brain and The Hormone Boys almost caused me an immediate creamy vomit. Wow oh wow, that was a burst of testosterone if I ever felt one.

When I saw daylight again I heard "My, you are horny, aren't you?"

Jason could barely keep me in check. Pattie got her answer by having me thrust forward into the very back of her throat. Jason didn't want to hold back; Pattie didn't want to hold back - and neither did I.

"FFFFAAAARRRRRRRRKKKKKKK!" cried Jason in as muffled and restrained a voice as he could control at that vital moment. I was sent into spasm, a creamy vomit free-fall. I'd already had an early morning session with Jason's hand so it wasn't that I was overloaded and needed an empty out, but with Pattie's physical mouth and hand being as soft and warm and tender as Jason had long imagined, the moment took over. Everything conspired to make that sweet-spot situation memorable - the danger, the imagination, the hormones, but especially the reality of being touched by a real-life, genuine, gorgeous, beautiful and sexy female. Her skin was warm, soft, pliable, amazing. Did I say, amazing? The first time touching of your sexual dreams in a real situation is never forgotten, and Pattie was giving Jason jack-off images for him to use for weeks to come.

As I was withdrawn I was somewhat embarrassed to see the sheer volume of teen-cream that I had deposited in her mouth and on her face. But I confess that I couldn't help it - The Hormone Boys and The Balls all conspired against me. I was helpless to maintain any sense of decorum or restraint. Hanging there in a limp and semi-deflated state I was still dripping when we heard the sound of someone else coming to the area and moving into an adjoining cubicle.

I was wiped dry on one of the clothing items that were there for being tried on. Pattie did the same to the remainder of the juice that she hadn't already swallowed. Jason pulled up his shorts from around his ankles.

With a huge smile on the face of both of them, Jason exited first. The area was clear and he discreetly moved across to wait near the bored boyfriend of the other cubicle occupier who was patiently waiting for his girlfriend's next clothing-to-be-revealed moment.

"I'll be down at Jackson's Bend on the river around three this afternoon – alone," she said to Jason as she swirled another new bikini past his gaze. "Bring beer and a packet of cock sox - and don't be late."

I think I dripped pre-cum virtually non-stop between the cubicle incident and the three o'clock rendezvous. Jason's mind was totally locked into Pussy Heaven, totally lost from the realities of the world. His constant erotic messages to me had me drip-feeding the front of his shorts with pre-cum, hence there was a constant wet spot for all to see. Having my head rubbed against the moisture did become somewhat even more stimulating before it became an annoyance.

"Fuck, man, what's that juice patch you're sporting?" Kyle said. "You've gotta learn to control those pocket billiard matches. I know it pays to advertise, but shit..."

With that very pointed observation from his friend, he decided that we'd better head for home before anyone else saw Wet Spot Central. There he could put me into some jocks and under a different pair of shorts. Then gather together the supplies that he would need for the afternoon's activities.

Lube, a brand new twelve pack box of condoms, beer, big towel, swimmers, sunscreen. As he gathered together the vital supplies he could only think of how momentous this day would be for him - his first intercourse, his first sex with a woman. How would it actually eventuate?

He was already surprised at how easy it was to find it (or more technically correct, how easily he was found by horny Pattie). She was older and more experienced, he knew that. And who had told her that his dick was big? Whoever it was, that was a great piece of public relations on their part. This morning's blow job was unexpected, though totally hoped for, and now she wanted to go further, the full nine yards. "Who would believe that getting your rocks off was this easy", he kept saying to himself. "This is going to be such a fucking good summer," he thought.

Jackson's Bend was a bit out of town, so a bike ride was the easiest way to get there. Not many townies made the journey to it, preferring to swim in the center of town at the pool. The young people knew that the more isolated the location, the better for making out with your latest date. There were lots of hidden areas where you could put down a towel and not be seen by anyone else. You could occasionally see nude swimming or watch couples necking in their private patch of ground under the branches of the low hanging trees. And occasionally hear moans and giggles of sexual pleasure taking place.

As you searched for an isolated play area, you could see used condoms, cigarette butts, beer cans - you know, the usual rubbish left by couldn't-care-less teenagers.

Jason and I found a good spot high up on the riverbank from where we could see anyone else who came to swim and where we couldn't easily be seen by them. Jason didn't want my activity to be witnessed by others, particularly as he was unsure how it was all going to go, this being the first time and all. There were a couple of others romping around in the water but they seemed not to care who else was in the vicinity.

The towel was already spread out on the ground by the time Pattie arrived. He waved and she made her way up to the eyrie with its isolation and grand view. Taking off her loose top she revealed her new two-piece bikini. At that sight, I was sent a "would-you-look-at-THAT" message from up above, along with a burst of energy to get me wide awake and alert. It was actually going to happen and he needed me ready for action.

They kissed long and wetly, though perhaps his inexperienced approach was more attack and confound, rather than passionate. But there was no denying Jason's enthusiasm for the task at hand. She slowed him down by reaching for a beer and daring him to get rid of all his clothes. This was good for me because I got to see first-hand what was ahead for me.

As she sipped and talked and laughed, she also discovered for the second time that day, my extensive delights. Her hand was drawn to me and she gently squeezed me into submission. The Balls got their squeeze first and didn't they like the closeness of her hand as it gently cupped them! They felt delighted and sent messages through to me that the entire team would be in for a treat VERY soon. Rather quickly, her hand moved on to my shaft and began to massage my length and polish my head. This was a wonderful experience for me as I'd so rarely been touched by the gentleness of a female hand. It was so different to the roughness of the boy's touch.

It wasn't long before the beer kicked in (or was it the testosterone-fueled eagerness of Jason) - either way, it had the same effect. I found myself being squashed between her now naked torso and Jason's crotch. How did that happen so fast? I was fully extended to my complete length, hard as a rock and already weeping tears of pre-cum on to her smooth and recently shaved lower reaches. As he lay on her, kissing her more and more intently, so I was rubbed up and down against her smooth skin. When he started kissing her breasts, he began a remote-control ploy to bring me in line with her already wet one-eyed undercarriage. His mental state was way ahead of the pack and overly eager to plunge into her. Any doubts that he had about my ability to perform under these conditions had quickly evaporated and he was more than aggressive about wanting me to move into her and show her that he was the stud that she hoped he would be.

As she squirmed under him she was feeling my head while I looked for that all-important Entrance to Paradise.

"Hold it Big Boy. You need a condom, remember? And some lube please!" stated Pattie.

As Jason fumbled for the latter his pressure on the tube was all too much. With one giant extruded dollop the gel covered his hand and dripped down on to her stomach.

"Fuck!", she exclaimed. "Well ok, finger me and put some into me and save some for the condom."

Unfortunately, Jason quickly became Mr. First-Fuck Fumble-Fingers. As it transpired, the combination and dexterity required to shift the beer can, handle the lube, finger Miss Pattie, open the cellophane cover of the condom box let alone tear open the condom's foil wrapping and roll the contents on to me, proved insurmountable. Arms, fingers, beer and additional splooged lube merged into one slippery catastrophe that saw me temporarily thrown from breast to kneecap. This was not in the least what The Boss had been fantasizing about for his first genuine fuck. As I saw it, what hapless lover DOESN'T open the cellophane wrapped condom box BEFORE any activity begins. That's Lesson#1, Jason!

There are few more dismal scenes than seeing a man

with lube-covered fingers trying to tear the cover off the condom pack. He's trying to look cool, experienced and in control of the situation when really he's silently crying out in shame and embarrassment at his ineptitude, hoping like hell that no-one was watching this miserable excuse for a sexual young man.

In between her fits of laughter, Pattie finally said to him "Give it to me". Sitting up, she saw that I was still proudly erect waiting for my moment to shine.

"Well, at least HE is still eager to fuck me" she joked as she tore open the individual condom sachet.

Jason was by this time on his knees, with me bolt upright looking at the sky.

"Bring him here" she ordered.

And with a deft hand, she placed it on my head, squeezed the condom teat to give me room to cough my juice into, and began the gentle roll down my shaft. Oh, man, was that a lovely gentle treat. That girl had learned her tricks from experts!

"Here, give me your hand" and had him wipe the excess lube all over my protective coat before getting him to place the remainder inside of her. I was now all dressed up and ready, and when I heard the low purring sounds emanating deep from within Jason, I knew that her hand wrapped around me was also transferring "fuck-me-soon, fuck-me-quick" messages to his brain. I could feel an urgency about it all and somehow I knew that those messages would be a foreboding of things to come.

As she lay on her back, legs apart, Pattie began to guide me like a GPS guidance system towards her waiting vagina. He began kissing her knowing that her directional skills were now homing me in on her motherlode. Through the blur of the sheath, I could see that I was being drawn closer and closer to ground zero. The area was wet, lubricated and waiting. Without a moment's hesitation, the message came down "we're going in buddy" - and in I went - all the way to the bottom of my shaft, somewhat squashing The Balls in the process. Obviously, Jason had NO intention of making this a long romantic interlude. This was Initiation 101, equivalent to the planting of the flag on top of Everest, the key to unlocking a long and happy sex life - and a celebration of his manhood emerging from childhood obscurity to teenage lust.

Pattie gave a quick but restrained gasp of surprise when she felt the full size of me inside of her. I was bigger than she had expected and I obviously caught her by surprise (she being the first of many over the following years who verbally expressed such audible approval). Still, she did have the foresight to remember to squeeze an internal muscle or two, and when she did, I transmitted that contraction straight to Jason.

Well, that sent him OVER THE TOP, didn't it!!!!! With only a few more thrusts, even though I was deep within Miss Pattie, I could hear the breathless anguished Masculine Moan of Sexual Abandonment.... "I'm cumming. I'm cumming. I'm C-U-M-M-I-N-G!!!!!!!!"

Jason had absorbed every one of those climax cries he'd heard on his porn and from that day forward, like every man anywhere in the world, the universal language of men climaxing became also part of his lexicon.

A final push, withdraw, push - and then I was over the top. Beyond control. I was totally unable to hold back from having massive muscle spasms that resulted in my juices thrusting outward to be captured in the teat, emptying my tanks to the last drop.

"FAAAARRRRKKKKKKK!!!!" was heard along the riverbank, with just one solitary "whoop" back in acknowledgment of a fellow fucker's achievements.

I was so copious that I thought that I'd start drowning in my own juices. My eye, my head, my upper shaft were all saturated with the thick warm juice. But I didn't have to stay in the dark for long.

I was unceremoniously pulled out and swayed from side to side. I could clearly see that Jason was over-the-moon with excited achievement and began to beat his chest in Tarzan-like actions.

"Look at me! Look at ME" his actions silently screamed out. With an additional punch into the air his moment of maturity, of becoming a true man, had been achieved and he was telling the world.

A "Good on ya buddy" came from down near the river's edge. "My turn next...?"

Naturally, I was still dripping the last of my juices and like a spider's web, strands of it drifted between me, Jason's leg and the smooth pubes of Pattie.

"Bit pleased with yourself?" asked Pattie.

"Fuckin' oath," he responded without a seeming care in the world for her. At that moment, it was all about Jason talking about himself - "ME. ME. ME"!

Well, really it wasn't about Jason at all. The "ME, ME, ME" was me, his penis. I was the worker, the one who transmitted all the satisfaction, who threw up a giant load of juice so that he could walk like a man.

"You are one fantastic shag" was all that could tumble out of his besotted mind. "Want to go again?"

"Ummm, Err Um, perhaps you might like to remove your remains from my pussy first."

"Why, what do you mean... remains?"

And then he looked down to discover the used condom emerging like a wrinkled cabbage from her patch. In his excitement to withdraw and because of my copiously juicy position, I had slipped out of my protection and flew straight up skywards attached to my deliriously happy owner. The condom containing all my juices remained inside. Well, I didn't know which way to look when he bent down and like a hesitant surgeon carefully removed it by giving it a generous tug. After flying through the air and hitting him in the chest it was just an unfortunate quirk of timing that my now cooled contents slipped backward from the used sheath and onto his chest and on to her leg. This sexual ineptness was simply all too much for Pattie to cope with.

Soon after, she packed up and left the scene of the sexual carnage and devastation - alone!

Jason and I spent the rest of the afternoon - and night - and for several weeks thereafter, dissecting and re-living his sexual rites-of-passage afternoon. Its memory provided untold opportunities to fuel his fantasies for wanking. In his mind the premature ejaculation upscaled into an ability for passionate lovemaking with multiple girls, the kissing became mutually desirable and the used condom incident segued into being a scenario of aggressive bareback sex with multiple climaxes during a long sex-fueled love-making afternoon.

By the time his class friends heard about the "Pattie Afternoon", the description was straight from a porn movie and bore no resemblance to a nervous kid's first time sexual adventure with all its abject failures and fumbling.

Those that had already been initiated into the delights of vaginal sex readily understood. No-one wanted to talk about reality. It was all about gross exaggeration and masculine bravado. The rites-of-passage sexual initiation separated the participant from idealistic youthful eagerness into the realms of manhood. Once you'd "done it" with a girl, all pretensions of childhood were swept away. You could now walk tall and be totally accepted by your like-minded buddies. Jason was now a man (well, technically still a bumbling teenager with an over-active dick) but together we were now a sexually rampant partnership, eager to bring pleasure to a supposedly desperate female world. What The Boss and I lacked in sexual experience, we made up for in ego, enthusiasm and wild flights of fantasy. It was all systems go from there on.

Sadly, I didn't get to enjoy the delights of Pattie ever again.

*"If sex with two people is called a twosome
and sex involving three is called a threesome,
now I understand why
I'm called handsome!"*

PETER BENN

CHAPTER TWO

MANSCAPING

My Jason does have hair on his body. Well, quite a lot of hair actually, especially in the lower reaches where I'm located. His upper torso has not so much. But you wouldn't know exactly how much he can naturally grow because shaving, trimming and waxing have at various times, all become a normal part of his life, thus disguising much of this hirsuteness.

These days he takes a lot more care about his body image as he's discovered that his lovers prefer the smoothness. In his younger days one young lady, as she picked stray hairs from her teeth, described him as a "fur-ball of epic proportions". This cat-like swipe at his masculinity took him days to get over. He simmered and stewed as if it had been a knife thrust deep into his young heart.

"Just about all guys have hair somewhere on their body" he muttered to his buddies. "It's just natural. What do these women expect from me? To be totally smooth and shaven all over? Trim the hair?"

"Just make the appointment Jason, and get yourself waxed. Bro, you'll come out a new man, and the women will totally fall for the new smooth look. What's a bit of pain for all the gain you'll get? They'll be lining up to run their hands all over smooth you."

Jason had already made one previous venture into this mysterious world of depilation which came as a total surprise to him and I might add, to me too.

This was back in his hairy, man-cave days when manscaping was not even a thought that ever entered his head. He was dating a vibrant young woman who was not only a fellow college student but a part-time model. And it was this latter work that attracted Jason to her, for she was simply a stunning beauty and she knew how to make her body totally attractive in every way.

As part of her job, she was accommodated in a five-star hotel across town so she invited Jason to share the night with her.

We'd had sex several times before but that night was different. The sex we had with her was full-on hot, steamy and amazing. It was the yin and yang of bodies, the smooth and the hairy. Each wanted something totally different to what they were themselves. It was a real-life scenario where opposites do attract. Both sought the pleasures that they didn't think were attractive in themselves.

However pleasurable it was, there had been pillow talk on a previous occasion about Jason's extremely hairy pubes and balls and she, who was as smooth as silk, thought that he might one day like to experience the pleasures of smoothness.

After that full night of pleasure and multiple orgasms, we headed to the shower and the bath, he the former, she the latter.

By that time of the morning, I was just hanging about somewhat exhausted and feeling used and abused as a good penis should when I heard her say,

"When you're finished your shower, come and join me in the bath. Run the shower good and hot so that your balls are all slack for me - and don't dry them off. I'll look after that part."

As you can imagine, I was intrigued. Anything that involved my pouched boys and a third party, always interested me, and if I might say, pricked my interest.

While her bath filled with warm water, she arranged one of the fluffy hotel towels onto the bathroom floor, placing a cake of soap and her ever-reliable woman's safety razor within easy reach.

As the shower had no walls to it I was able to watch all this happening. Jason was just as intrigued as he sensed that both he and I were in for a shaving experience the like of which we hadn't participated in before.

We stepped out of the shower and Jason dried his upper torso. The water had been extremely hot so I really did hang down like a wet rag on a summer's day. The Balls were in their carry bag, which was as loose as stretched elastic.

With soap in hand, she came to us. She lathered it between her hands and then clasped me and my two friends, covering us with a generous layer of the slippery substance.

"On your side, on the towel" she ordered. His head rested on a second folded and rolled towel.

"Your hands. Put them together" and with that, she tied them together with a scarf we hadn't noticed she had nearby.

"What..." exclaimed Jason.

"Just do as I tell you. You'll love the experience all the more if you can't touch yourself. Now roll onto your back."

Jason obliged.

The hot water was running in the hand basin heating up the razor.

With a third towel under her knees, razor now in hand, she gently lifted my length upright by holding me firmly by my head. This, of course, had an immediate reaction from my master, who now, hog-tied and with somewhat restricted movement, started pumping additional blood into me.

"Good boy!" she exclaimed, looking directly at me. "Aren't you the turned-on one - and I haven't even started yet!"

It was true. The feeling of being restricted AND having someone else take charge of the moment was an immediate turn-on like he'd never experienced before in his youthful sex life. In only a matter of moments, there was no need for her to hold me upright - I was very capable of pointing to the ceiling without any assistance.

"OOOhhhhh" I cried out to myself. "OOOOh-hhhhhhhh........"

The smooth first stroke of the blade was intoxicating as it glided along the shaft removing those sparse single hairs that seemed to grow out of it for no reason. Then around the tufts where the pubes and my shaft co-habit. It was a little tougher going there, but her deft hand soon denuded the area so that you could see very clearly where I emerged from his skin.

With one hand, she pulled the scrotum upwards so that the skin became quite taught and with the razor hand, began the scrape through the wiry and hairy wilderness that had been foresting Jason's dangling manhood since puberty had hit.

The combination of soap lather and razor, together with such a skilled operator, soon had Jason cooing with contentment. He tried to sit up and take a look at what was happening to me and his beloved balls, but with the tied hands that was not to be.

"Just lie back and let it happen" she responded. "You don't want me to cut you, do you?"

Indeed, I didn't want her to do that either. This, my initiation into smooth ball-sac territory, was so.... so.... OOOOhhhhhhhhh - sensual!!!! I'd not experienced anything like it ever before. It was like being reborn. Like an explorer emerging from the thick jungle into a sun-drenched clearing. Like a fresh-faced newborn baby. Like the shine on a Number 8 snooker ball.

Jason writhed and cooed and ground his butt into the

towel, and all the while I looked skyward doing my own pleasurable oohing and aahing.

"Now the pubes.... Now... those pubes" she repeated to herself. With a hand towel rinsed in hot water, she wet the remaining hairy wilderness, generously lathered it up with the soap, rinsed the razor and went on the attack. She told us that she would have liked to have trimmed back the length of the pubic hair before beginning, but what-the-heck, let's do it anyway, she concluded.

The scraping sound behind where I was upright sounded intense, to say the least. You've seen the movies where the jungle adventurer hero uses a machete to rip the thick jungle foliage apart, well, that was the scene there on the hotel bathroom floor that morning. The scene had moved from ball sac sensuality to practical harvesting methods of the threshing variety. Like tall forest timbers, the hairs were felled, like tangled ropes on a yacht they hurt as they pulled and stretched against one another.

I was quickly subsiding! Jason's mind had obviously moved from "this-girl-can-do-no-wrong" to "what-the-fuck-does-she-think-she's-doing" mode. But he was going nowhere, bound that he was and having her sitting on his legs while performing her deforestation.

I slumped back to my casual limp position just in time to watch it taking place. There was going to be a total hair eradication right down to where I emerge from his lower body. In a very short time from amidst the lather and the sacrificed hair, there emerged a distinctly different man – a BALD one!

Balls, shaft, and pubes were as much as she wanted to do that day. But it was enough to give Jason and me a totally new experience - and a new look, a manly make-over.

"Back in the shower and wash off" she ordered as she untied him. "Let me see what my handiwork achieved."

And with that, she turned off the now filled warm bath and climbed into it.

"Hey model boy, bring that nice dick over here and let me admire."

As he stepped from the shower both he and I had that great "Look at me. LOOK AT ME" feeling. Remember getting that first bike and you wanted to show it off to everyone, so you immediately took it for a spin? Well, Jason and I felt exactly the same way. He felt so extraordinarily excited and different, especially after he caught a look at himself in the mirror. His horniness grew sky high. Between the shower and the bath, I got the message - let's show her what a "bald" college boy can do when buried deep within a smooth college girl.

And that we did. Now that I and my undercarriage purse were as smooth as the proverbial baby's bottom and surrounded by skin that I hadn't seen in years, I was greatly admired by his shave lady. Freshly showered, Jason slipped into the bath and it was Passion Central from the first moment.

Fortunately, I don't need oxygen, so being plunged into a warm bath proved to be no obstacle for me, stiff and ready for action that I was. After the first wild groping and kissing, she directed him to sit on the edge of the bath so that I could be viewed up close, all smooth and tempting. After briefly admiring her handiwork and telling Jason what a stud he now looked, her lips locked on to me. The languid and exhausted Jason that had awoken only an hour before was now fully recovered and he kept sending me messages of enjoyment every time her mouth and/or tongue moved about my length.

So, there I was getting frantic messages of "I love it, I love it - but don't blow just yet" from the guy upstairs and there she was, pleasuring my outside skin and nerve ends moaning "Mmm Mmmm Mmmm". My mind was caught up in a whirlwind of sensations. My man hadn't been this horny in many weeks.

Just when he thought all control was about to be lost, she releases me, stands up, spreads the body wash liquid into her glorious shaved cavity, grabs the sides of the bath with both hands and gives him the message he'd been hoping for. I took a final look at the bath scene, stiffened my erection muscles and, as she lowered herself on to me, in I went - with no "beg-your-pardons".

What a workout we had together! It was wet, intense, quick and immensely pleasurable for all concerned. Well, truth be, for me at least, apricot scented body wash liquid isn't as enjoyable as some of the other body lubricants but hey, it served the purpose without breaking the lust that was reeking-havoc that morning between the two of them. Of course, with no condoms in sight, was I going to shoot inside or was I going to cloud the water?

He gave me no indication - until I could hold back no longer. Into her recesses, I sent my seed, spurt after spurt, spasm after spasm. Oh, it was dark and sticky and very apricot perfumed but I've been in worse situations. I was ordered to stay there as long as I could, but truth be known, I was exhausted and when that happens, I quickly move toward the limp end of the scale.

She lifted herself off me, releasing Jason from his position under her and therefore also releasing me back into the warm bathwater. I began to float and enjoy the sensations of near weightlessness. This was penis heaven - a good intense workout followed by a relaxing spa.

But it didn't last. Suddenly, my daydreaming was rudely and unexpectedly interrupted as I was thrust up and out of the water as Jason stood up. And then I began to hear the dialogue....

"Did you just fuckin' cum inside of me you little shit?"

"Sure babe. It's what you wanted, wasn't it?"

"Like, no, it wasn't. We'd agreed that we'd play safe. Trust me, I don't want to get pregnant, and certainly not to you."

"But you were screaming your tits off wanting me to screw you deeper."

"Jeez, Jason, sometimes I think that you're ruled by that prick of yours. Your brains are in your dick!"

Well, like any highly skilled athlete or gym junkie I like being admired and talked about - but this seemed to be going too far. Or at least Jason thought so. For me, there was more than an element of truth in her accusation as I do have certain skills and nerve endings whereby I *can* push Jason to pleasurable limits he has no control over. That's part of my job specifications and at nineteen years of age, he still had a lot to learn from me about self-control versus over-enthusiasm.

"That's unfair and you know it," he said, trying to defend his youthful impetuousness and that really he was just a testosterone filled guy at the height of his exuberant horniness.

"Well, you can just take that cum-filled out-of-control dick right out of my life and fuck-off for good. And if I'm pregnant you'll hear about it. Now get out of here. Right now, you sleaze bucket!"

Well, there's nothing worse than not being talked about, and I was sure in the firing line that morning. At least I wasn't being overlooked.

With a heavy heart, Jason dried himself, packed me into his jocks in the folded-under position (just as if we were a cowering animal leaving with its tail between its legs), and we departed the scene of what had been up until then, an immensely enjoyable twelve-hour period together in that hotel room.

We departed the lobby and began the drive home. I slumbered peacefully in the warm environs of Jason's groin, enjoying lying over the smooth skin of what was an hour or two ago his hairy jungle. It was a little stickier than I'd been used to as the hair would allow some air to move around and keep my skin from sticking to his groin. But right then neither of us cared too much - or so I thought.

He planned to drive the long way home - along the beach boulevard. It was one of his favorite places to look at the girls in their skimpy beachwear and many a time he had scored a date from there. He stopped and parked the car, walked to the beach wall and surveyed the scene. It didn't take long for his sex-magnet radar to hone-in on three beautiful girls sunning themselves on the beach. With a "wake-up-down-there" twitch to me, we were off on another adventure. It was going to be the continuation of a long and very busy forty-eight hours, though this time with a twist – freshly shaved pubes and polished balls.

Now, who could resist a playdate with us – Mr. Jason Cool and his Best Friends, Smoothie McBigBoy and his twin associates, Ball Buster Bertie and Private Bollocks?

Or resist a pickup line as good as "Yeah. Just shaved the carpet from the old lunchbox love muscle and it's ripe for some coochie action right now. Play your cards right and you can all have my bobby dangler in your bat cave before the hour is up?"

And indeed, we did pull (though how on earth he managed to do so with that and similar absurd and politically incorrect obscenities, I'll never know), spending a delightful afternoon back at our place showing off our smoothness to the two sisters and their mid-twenties interstate blonde friend.

******

"Whoa, bro! If you keep scratchin' "Down There" the chicks will think you've got crabs" said Mick. "That's not the best look when you're aimin' to score."

It took a quite a few days for the pubic growth to begin to sprout again but like cactus after a rainfall, sprout it did - and at a furious rate. But it was my sac that seemed to be the most fertile region for regrowth. Who knew!

With the whole groin area now as itchy as hell, not only was I on edge but so was my host. Every brush with clothing made him want to scratch a little more. As the sac grew spikier so the tough little hair re-growths pushed into the jock fabric and sent messages northward that reminded Jason that he was going through a form of torture brought about by what he called "the bitch from the bath" (he still hadn't actually got over being dumped by her) and never missed an opportunity to tell anyone who would listen about her "over-reaction" to his hot sexual advances. All his drinking mates in the bar knew the full shaving story and in some instances, were actually decidedly impressed, wishing it had been them in the situation. Naturally, *they* would have had better self-control and pulled out before cumming and kept the relationship humming along!

But right at this moment, Jason was declaring that he'd never shave again because the prickling was becoming unbearable. Our sex over the last couple of nights reinforced the fact that the new growth was too much like razor wire for him to endure.

With one partner, he stopped sex in mid-flight, the other he refused point blank to let continue any further than a blowjob. It was clearly becoming decision time - no sex for a couple of weeks until regrowth was beyond the bristled lawn scenario or - out with the razor and soap, and man-up to doing it himself on a regular basis.

Recalling that the three beach girls had all devoured me and seemed very impressed with Jason's smoothness, around 3am the decision was made. He couldn't sleep because (1) of the itchiness, and (2) that night he was (unusually) sleeping alone. That was the double whammy that turned him into a regular shaver. During all this, I was dangling freely as he couldn't any longer cope with any clothing around his spikiness.

3.01am -
on to YouTube for a look at the pubic shaving videos.

My, my - there were such a lot of different techniques. Under the shower, over the bathroom basin, sitting on the toilet, even lying on the bed. I saw it all and hoped beyond hope that he would have a steady hand. I'm not good with blood, especially when it's from *my* part of the body.

3.33am -
layout the implements, get under the shower, warm up and soften the sprouting hairs....

3.41am -
"Well, Big Boy, it's time! Sorry man, I'll try not to cut you, but here goes...."

With lights blazing, hot water running, soapy lathering happening, towels at the ready, new razor in hand, he began his first solo attempt at self-beautification.

The first area to attack was the "Field of Thorns", that patch of ultra-annoying pubic hair that had sprouted across his lower stomach area and was causing him unbearable intimate itch. While the skin was still warm from the shower, the field was soaped-up to a lather and the first strike moment arrived.

Though I couldn't see everything in the mirror from my dangling position I could see what looked like a soapy re-enactment of a gruesome Hollywood war epic. From the shouting going on above me you'd think that this man had never shaved before. Gingerly, he eyed up the field he was about to make a path through, lowered the blade to near where my length emerged from his body, took an audibly loud deep breath, and began the scrape northward towards his navel.

"Shiiiiiiiiitttttt!!!!" was the cry that emanated from deep

within his chest.

"Fuck man, look at that," he said looking down at me in amazement as he saw the first smooth-skinned pathway through the stubble and the soapy lathering. "Oh fuck, that feels so bloody good."

I wondered what I was to do in order to look at this miraculous happening - unscrew myself and jump up on the sink and applaud!!!!! It was, after all, just another shave job, just not on the face. But reassurance to him at this highly emotional time of self-discovery seemed to be important. Hence I sent my congratulations via a quick tweet up the nervous system reminding him that I was still there and appreciating what he was doing for our future sex lives.

"Thanks, Big Buddy - I got that one." And tweaked a tingle back again. I was starting to grow.

"There - look at that," he said, as he triumphantly wiped away the last of the soapy residue. "Who wouldn't want to play with me now? So, Big Guy, it's your turn to shape up and shine."

He continued by wetting the soap and applying it all around The Balls. Holding me by the head, upright and toward the freshly mown patch, he rinsed the razor and began to shave me. Now, he's seen me a million, zillion times, but I reckon that he's never taken much notice of the pliable purse holder hanging beneath me. I mean, in the heat of summer I let my ball holder stretch to its limit and somewhat smooth out while The Balls try to cool themselves down, and in the winter - the opposite. I scrunch up the purse really tightly so that there's warmth for them, but that also means that it's got heaps of crease lines.

So, what's he trying to do here? He needs to stretch the purse a little so that there's a smooth surface to run the razor along.

In his first attempt, I sent a very abrupt signal to him to be more careful. My sac is not to be damaged. With two more jump-start messages that flinched my very being, he finally remembered what happened that morning on the bathroom floor. Yep - stretch then shave, stretch then shave.

I have to give him credit, that once he did remember the procedure, he was VERY careful with me and The Balls. Holding me this way, then that way, he managed to get into all the nooks and crannies around the shaft as well as on the sac.

Gently he wiped off the harvested hair and the soap, stood proudly in front of the full-length mirror and there I was in all my bald glory shining like a dance-floor mirror ball. The still hairy legs and the hairy chest helped contrast his smooth pubes and my enticing charms. It also made me look HUGE! Well, at least a whole lot larger than what I normally look. Ok, ok, ok - a BIT bigger at least!

I swelled with pride as he admired me and then held me in his hand. It was time for some lube to go into that hand and some quick exercise of the satisfying creamy eruption variety before a short but good night's sleep to follow.

Summer was barely underway and with this new found sexual freedom The Boss had discovered it was going to be a VERY busy one for me - I could sense it in my shaft!

Goodbye itch, hello girls.

Now, all these years later, we continue to shave The Balls but only trim the pubes. Having some trimmed fuzz lets Jason believe that it's much more masculine - and what's more, the women like it too!

And while we're on this manscaping theme, let me tell you all about... THE FIRST WAXING!!!

"Why do guys say that masturbation under the shower is so good?

Don't you get your laptop wet?"

PETER BENN

CHAPTER THREE

JASON'S MANZILIAN

One of Jason's more intellectual bedmates (well before the aforementioned Miss Bath Bitch of 2003) referred to the warm hairy nest that surrounded me as a "corncob lost in a sea of wild oats".

"What an insult to my manly attributes" was my first reaction to that, especially when it was obvious for all to see that HER attributes could have also done with a mowing. I well remember that as I was pushed forward through her wilderness, I barely had time to avoid her chrome vulva ring from poking me in the eye. One likes to have notice of such impending disasters before they happen from out of nowhere, especially as there are times when the upper guidance system, often blindly directed by Jason, leaves a lot to be desired. I'm usually just pushed and directed through feel rather than by a firm guiding hand who visually knows exactly where he is going with me. While he concentrates on his kissing and fondling I'm left to fend for myself and hopefully by some mysterious serendipity I find her welcome opening all by myself. But when there's the additional surprise of jewelry hidden amidst the undergrowth, then more care should be taken by all humans concerned with the act of consummation.

"Everything off please - including the jocks," said Maria, the head beautician. "And don't be embarrassed, we've seen it all before. Every shape and size have passed through my hands at some time or other. And still, they come back for more" she laughed in what Jason interpreted as an evil, tortuous payback to mankind.

"And please, no cracking a fat," said Jason's mate Toby from behind the video camera. The other guys in the drinking group wanted video of their mate being tortured by the waxing experience, so Toby was the chosen one to accompany him on this exercise and collect for posterity every scream, wince and "what-the-fuck" that would be uttered. The guys had done this same exercise with other group members and afterward spent many hysterical nights sharing the resulting videos with others in the bar. They knew that Jason was a bit of a "screamer" with a lower than usual pain threshold, so they were expecting good video mileage from today's waxing.

"I can assure you, Jason, that a cracking of the fat as your friend would say, will not happen for you. Though, if you feel the urge, do go right ahead. I can see with what I'm holding that you must be very popular with the ladies - and perhaps with the gentlemen too" she added through more self-deprecating laughter and titillating innuendo.

Toby was thrilled to have captured this first video gem for the day as he knew the latter reference to Jason's (unproven) popularity or "just curious experimentation" with men would cause much hilarity on the replays.

Even though the salon was warm, Maria's hand on me wasn't as warm as I would have liked - so no erection signal from Jason. The Boss was lying on his back looking upwards to the ceiling acting all nonchalant as if this was an everyday event and that it would just be a mere formality, a quick necessary inconvenience that would be over and done within no time at all.

She moved me to face south, towards his feet, as she was going to wax his pubes first, followed by The Balls and then do the chest, back, crack and legs.

The container holding the hot wax arrived and Maria put on the gloves, dipped the spatula into the molten syrup and spread the first golden mass across part of his pubes.

"Awww shit. That's hot, hot, HOT!!!!"

And with that momentary exclamation, the event moved from calm "what's-all-the-fuss-about" to "hellfire-and-damnation-at-the-doorway-to-Hades".

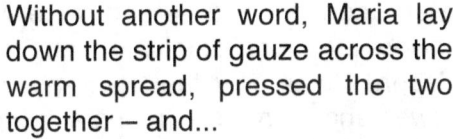

Without another word, Maria lay down the strip of gauze across the warm spread, pressed the two together – and...

"Three. Two. One..." chirped in a very excited Toby, knowing full-well that the next second was going to make all the filming very worthwhile. It was the moment of truth. Maria pulled back the strip...

"FFFFFFAAAAAAAARRRRRRKKKKKKK!!!!!!!!!!"

The scream could have been heard two states away. Jason's body arched high off the bench. I was flung violently from side to side as his body lurched like a New Age guru walking on hot coals for the first time. His eyes very nearly popped out of their sockets. The legs flayed out uncontrollably, very nearly making a home-run into Toby's scrotal ballpark. And if I didn't know better, we almost had to scrape his fingernails out of the ceiling where they lodged when he flung himself skywards.

"Oh, dear God" he added through intense moments of breathlessness. "That was A-W-F-U-L!!!"

Toby was jumping with glee, barely able to keep his hand steady enough to continue the filming of this auspicious, perhaps never-to-be-repeated event. Jason's reaction had gone w-a-a-a-a-a-y beyond what he had expected to film. This was video gold at its finest! He could barely contain his excitement knowing how well that reaction would go down with the guys at the bar. Jason would be buying drinks for everyone in order for the video to be stopped being shown.

Maria continued to spread more wax on the pubes, followed by more defoliation and more screaming from Jason. I was now feeling some of this fiery hell at the lower end of my shaft where there were bushy tufts of pubic hair from which I emerged.

The first lathering of the hot wax lava on the area sent me into spasm. "Oh fuck, oh fuck, fuck, fuck, f-a-r-k" I silently cried as my whole willy length was flung violently from side to side by The Boss in some desperate attempt to avoid the immediate pain and the impending doom.

1-2-3 – R-I-PPPPPPPPP!!!!!!!!

"AAAARRRRRGGGGGGHHHHHHH!!!!!!! Oh, my God. Oh, man!!!!!" came the next anguished cry from Jason - but what the fuck about ME!

This meeting place where his hairy pubes used to grow and where my shaft begins was right then screaming pain like a million bees had just stung the area. It was ragingly hot as if a military scorched-earth scenario had been acted out upon me. I glanced a quick look at the devastation. The skin was blotchy, bright red like the backside of a monkey on heat – and I was NAKED! Not a single wiry hair to be seen. I was as hair-free as the day I was born. Let me assure you that it was not at that moment, a pretty sight. It was indeed, total Apocalyptic desolation.

Then the other side was done with more of the same devastatingly, agonizing torture. One hoped that Jason would never – ever - consider doing this again to me, though I had heard the guys talking about having it done every two months or so. That's six times a year, sixty times a decade, maybe that's TWO HUNDRED AND FORTY times over the next forty years. Holy Moly! Little wonder that I shriveled up even more at that very thought.

As his buns, back and legs were defoliated I felt every intense muscle contraction, every total body convulsion and heard EVERY scream. Jason was not having a fun time and that was being transmitted throughout his body. I was not immune from the intense streams of "what-the-fuck" pulsing throughout his body. He knew full well that this waxing was like an initiation ceremony, a coming-of-age moment, a time when he had to prove to his masculine peers that he too was one of them and could endure the Fires of Hell just as well as they had done.

"And now we shall finish off with The Balls" continued Maria. Toby was still delirious with glee over what reactions he had already captured and was now hoping for at least one more scream of pain with the nut-sack hair clearance. And as for me – well, I was bracing myself for a tidal-wave of pain to come from the epicenter of that extraction, The Balls.

I felt Maria's now warm hand gently lift me up on to the devastated wasteland where Jason's pubes once flourished. I needed to be out of the way so that this last outpost of The Hirsute Empire could be attacked. It would be the conclusion to an epic defoliation exercise.

Her gentle squeeze momentarily diverted my attention from the impending doom, so much so that I gave a flicker of growth.

"Ah hah" Maria responded. "Your big boy is telling me that he's ready for some hanky-panky action as soon as you leave here. That would be a lucky girl, but I'm sorry to tell you that you cannot do that. Your friend here behind the camera knows from his waxing that you cannot have sex during the next twenty-four hours."

Jason was devastated. He didn't go through all this painful beautification not to use it as a chick-magnet lure from the moment he walked out of the salon's door. On hearing that I quickly returned to my limp state.

"And no gym workout, hot-tubbing or swimming. You don't want to risk getting an infection" she added.

TINDERfella

As I learned later, Toby captured the close-up shot of Jason's disappointment on hearing that news. When it was screened to the boys at the bar they soaked up every minute of Jason's agony and disappointment. Toby's camerawork captured every "Blair Witch" scream and every "Halloween" scare reaction. It was priceless.

But nothing previously videotaped matched the dramatic finale between the tangled hairy Captain Ballsac and the hair-hating, hands-on, ball-teasing Sister Maria, The Man-Waxing Tyrant of Salon d'Ecstacy.

It was not a long battle but it was a gothic horror moment just the same. Jason was on his back, his knees up, The Balls in all their hairy finery totally exposed to the invading elements. Both sides of this battle took up positions. The camera was rolling. The last of the hot wax in the pot was ready. The all invasive super-weapon, the spatula was primed.

With a deft sleight-of-hand, the spatula of hot wax made its mark. It hit and covered The Balls with its hot sticky lava-like properties, enmeshing the multitude of hairy tendrils within its sticky grasp. I felt the air escape Jason's throat and his stomach arch in preparation for the impending 1-2-3. I too reacted to the fiery heat attack by zapping back to minuscule length.

With a take-no-prisoners attitude, the dreaded Maria went straight for the proverbial jugular. The multiple strips of cloth met the waiting wax and without any mention of a 1-2-3, she pulled them skywards.

Did the video lens crack? The windows of the salon shatter? Eardrums burst? Very, very nearly!
Jason had saved the very best scream for the climax. If you were in the waiting room or a passerby outside, you

would have instantly known that the Torture Chamber from Hell was here and in action in this very establishment. You would not wait around to discover any more. Whatever it was that now lived in the Salon d'Ecstacy it was far, far worse than anything ever imagined in a movie.

"AAAAAAAAAAAAAHHHHHHHHHHHHHHHH!!!!!!!
Oh, Fuck. Shit. Shit. Fuck. Oh, Hell. Oh, man... I'M NEVER FUCKING EVER, EVER, EVER DOING THIS AGAIN you hear" my master cried out, nay roared out, in total agony.

"Worse than having a baby I guess" chimed in a totally hysterical Toby, trying to make light of the situation and to keep the camera rolling despite falling about with laughter.

Again, absolutely no concern for me and what was actually happening down my way. There I was in the epicenter of this capitulation to the forces of wax and devastation, feeling every molecule of pain that shot out of The Balls and throughout Jason's entire nervous system. Let me tell you that there's nothing quite like a bolt of pain to shoot right through one's shaft to cause untold shrinkage and shock. Bloody hell, those Balls must have been hard-wired into Jason's everything as they gave the biggest discharge of painful electricity imaginable. If you've been accidentally hit in your own gonads by a fast traveling ball or uncontrolled foot, then imagine that pain ten times over and you have some idea of what it was like for me.

As I quietly surveyed the situation it was post-apocalyptic in nature. All around was the now barren parched hairless skin of Jason. Where the pubes once flourished, there was nothing – absolutely nothing but scorched red skin. His chest was now smooth and white from the talcum powder sprinkled on it. The legs were as smooth as those on a professional cyclist. The Balls and their purse had changed from fur-like to silk-like. My shaft now had continuous skin from cock-head to his pecs, from shaft to his toes - with not a single missed hair to indicate what had proudly grown there minutes before.

As Jason rose from the table I could see that the event had drawn quite a group of onlookers.

"Who's next?" inquired Maria, as the watching group murmured, then quietly and cowardly dispersed.

As his body started to calm down I did feel a new sense of freedom, of being ready for new skin-to-skin sensations. I did pride myself on looking even larger now that part of me was no longer hidden by the hairy acreage behind me. With a beer or two inside, Jason also began to take pride in his new smooth look.

"Well, buddy," he said aloud, looking down at me. "Bugger this waiting for twenty-four hours. Let's go off and pick up right now. We need to get value for all that pain. And get you hard and working. You might look like a deserted wiener on a shiny new plate but who cares. So long as we pull... And .... you do look bigger than I think you did when I had hair? Or am I just imagining that?"

I smiled inwardly knowing that the sexual action after the forthcoming nightclub visit was going to be vintage Jason and me. Right now, though, we were two hairless buddies on the prowl for new admirers. There was an immediate stiffening at the very thought of what delightful pussy action we would find that night.

It's only four inches –

but then some girls like it that wide!

PETER BENN

CHAPTER FOUR

EUROPEAN VACATION

"Four weeks. As many countries as we can visit. Shag as many girls as we can."

If Jason and Andrew had written their own travel brochure it would have started something like that. It was their gap year between college and starting a proper job, and they - and that meant me too - headed off to sunny Europe where a million or more hot vaginas were hopefully waiting to be discovered and pleasured. Indeed, the odd bricks and mortar tourist attraction would also help the boys add to their somewhat limited cultural knowledge but more importantly, it was a sure place to pick up chicks from all manner of exotic international backgrounds.

PARIS
We'd barely gotten off the plane before I was put on by a pair of air hostess lips in a quiet part of the terminal near the crew station. Jason and the blonde had chatted on board but had to wait until she'd been signed off duty and we'd cleared customs. Was it just an accident that she spilled champagne on his crotch and then had to sponge him dry with a cloth? While diligently doing her

duty, and apologizing profusely, her hands found a way to manipulate me to much more than a semi-rigid state. With that, Jason and I both knew that we couldn't clear the terminal without at least a good blow job. Andrew looked after the bags and admired the passing parade of feminine opportunity in the arrivals-lounge while I was sucked and licked and vacuumed clean. Oh, such a warm welcome to Europe.

"Does a blowjob count?" asked Andrew "you know, on the Pussy Scoresheet? Or is it only when we do the complete dirty?"

This was important to get clear from the beginning, as competition between the two to bed the most girls in four weeks was going to be very intense.

"How about if a filled beaver gets a full point whereas a BJ only rates half," responded Jason.

"Definitely. Let's count everything towards that final score" responded Andrew.

With that important clarification now agreed, and with our first half point already topping the scorecard, it was on to the backpacker's hostel.

Money was going to be a bit tight on this trip, so sharing digs with like-minded other young backpackers would be common for us. That meant shared rooms with other guys, shared facilities and no secrets when it comes to the main purpose of the vacation - booze and chick sex.

That first night in Paris found Andrew and Jason wandering the Marais area. Lots of little meandering back streets with their bar patrons sitting outside in the warm night air, lots of laughter and lots of easy conversation with passers-by. To get a drink at the Grosse Bite Bar (the Big Cock Bar or Big Prick if you'd rather - and yes, there was a rooster symbol attached to the name) was a push and shove maneuver for one of the guys to get to the actual bar, and with an equally delicate balancing trick to get the drinks back outside to the table. But they managed and soon had joined an extended table of revelers, some of whom they recognized from the backpacker hostel and some who were local.

Andrew was soon attaching himself to a quirky girl from Britain - "I just adore the British accent" he kept saying to her. "Tell me something really dirty so that I can hear it sound so interesting..."

But Jason had eyes for Monique, a Parisian local who particularly liked male tourists. After much drinking, Andrew headed back to the hostel with his new friend while Jason and I headed back to the apartment of Monique. It was on a side street and up several flights of stairs. I didn't have to see it to know what was happening. I could hear the intermittent conversation in-between bouts of being groped as we walked along the cobblestoned street and being pressed like a can of sardines against her pussy as we drunkenly clambered the tight staircase and body surfed on every landing. I was already erect, so no issues in that department − the pressure just intensified my pleasure.

We'd barely got inside the door of the apartment before Jason was madly kissing her all over, removing her small amount of summer clothing at the same time. If this encounter had happened a few years later then there would have been much more seduction, more erotic pleasuring, but as a hot-blooded young man let loose in horny Europe there was none of that. Because of the heat, I'd been free-balling inside Jason's shorts.

With all the haste, I soon got to see the natural beauty of young Monique and I could see why he was so impressed. Tight breasts, slim curves, hairless smooth skin from neckline to ankle strap.

After a session of intense nipple licking it was time to head south for Jason to spend a few moments on his knees enjoying his first fine French cuisine. Eating out a French local was going to be just as enjoyable as it was back home. My job was to stay erect and look at the side of the bed until I was called. Some gentle handwork from The Boss as he chowed deeper kept nudging me along and making me feel really good.

It was only after a couple minutes of this fine dining that The Balls felt something move along beneath them and they telegraphed it to me. I hadn't seen it sneaking up from behind me, but when a wet nose and then a rough wet tongue landed SLOSH against my eye and head I reeled back in sudden astonishment. More telegraphing of messages - this time straight up to The Boss.

"URGENT. URGENT! – WE HAVE IMMINENT INTERRUPTUS!"

He lifted his head from his savory macaron and looked down to see a small white dog using me as a tasting stick – or more precisely, a licking stick, a bone already! Jason jumped back a little, surprised at the unexpected intruder and realizing what the strange sensation that the raspy tongue was providing actually was. In fact, he found it quite erotic, even if somewhat unconventional. VERY different to a smooth human mouth.

"Ahhh Fifi, my darling, you've found my jolly Jason" and with that Fifi bounded up into her owner's arms.

LICKED BY A DOG!!!!!! I could hardly believe it – it was so humiliating. This is something I'll need to keep to myself I thought, though knowing Jason, everyone would know about it by morning. Oh, the shame of it all!

I'd barely come to grips with holding on to my suddenly wilting erection when she added: "and where's Oscar?"

Well, The Boss was quickly able to answer that...

"I think it's him that's licking my butt..."

And his message down to me was "what the fuck is going on here?"

I wilted even more. Both Jason and I had been usurped by her love for her dogs. As she lay back naked on the bed, her legs still spread, she was happy to be licked on her face by both the canines. She indicated to Jason to get back to work on her pussy. It was as if nothing had changed for her - but for us it had. Neither Jason nor myself like playing second fiddle in the bedroom. We're both proud of our looks, our technique and our total dedication to the task at hand, but when we're ignored then - that's it! It's all over, red rover.

Jason decided it was time to leave and couldn't even bring himself to give her a kiss on her now wet canine-licked face. A quick peck on the top of her head and we were off out the door.

I was still full of pressure from the build-up created further up the fuel line, so something had to give before sleep. As we tried to induce sleep in the bunk, we could hear Andrew slowly humping his girl which only made me hornier. As she continued her slow relentless noisy ride to orgasm I was treated to a hand-job. As we'd dipped out on dick penetration (tongue dipping and taste twaddling were not included in the score chart) we were now half a point behind Andrew in the girl-bedding stakes. But that was only day one. There was always tomorrow.

"Yeah, one licked the end of my dick and the other my ass" blabbed Jason to the amused group having their petite déjeuner of cheese, ham, and croissant. I was humiliated, as he should have been too, but there are no secrets with The Boss.

"I thought that getting a cramp was a turnoff, but hey, that's priceless" added a guy from the group, all of whom were vainly trying to outdo the others with their own sex tale exploits from the night before.

"I had no trouble when she brought out the whip" spruiked another. "I just got harder."

"And that's why you're standing up to eat. Right?" suggested a third, thus instigating more laughter all around.

With that, Whip Man simply smiled, dropped his shorts and mooned the group at the table displaying an impressive range of very red welts across his buttocks.

"WHOA buddy" another responded in horror. "That's awful. That must hurt like shit, man."

"Definitely – but I loved every fuckin' minute of it. Tied to the bedhead I couldn't have escaped anyway. But yeah, it was a bit raw under the shower but you gotta try everything you know... She gave me the best orgasm..."

As I strained to see the world through Jason's shorts I could just make out the redness and it kind of made our own doggie escape seem a little pitiful by comparison.

That night the hostel back garden was going to be turned into party central with a swimsuit or underwear party. I could feel Jason's twitches already priming me. Would we have a better story to share tomorrow morning? Only time would tell.

ROME

Rome was a totally sensuous city. It was as if romance and sexuality oozed from every sun-drenched brick, fountain or parkland. The heat of high summer just added to the horniness that invaded Jason's body and hence into me too. It slowed us down and forced us to take long rests in shaded corners of the city, both old and new. The heady aroma of jasmine mingled with those of pasta sauces and the smell of car exhausts. It let you know that this was a city to relax in, to take the time to look at and appreciate the antiquities. And, of course, to make love to beautiful women, not like a zippy motor scooter but like a slow horse and carriage ride.

It was in the huge parkland of the Villa Borghese in the center of Rome that we had our first encounter. It was mid-afternoon, the heat was intense, the cool surrounds of the lake were enticing. Andrew and Jason were thinking of cold beers when they saw two attractive young women sharing a cake while sitting beside the lake.

"Buongiorno," said Andrew. "Isn't it so hot?" he added in his native English.

"Where are you from?" came the reply - and so it was that conversation ensued. What to see, what we had seen, best places for meeting people - you know, all the usual tourist/locals type small talk.

"Where can we go that's cool?" asked Jason.

"We live just over from the main south entrance near Via Vittoria Veneto. Would you like to come and have a cool drink with us?"

And so, the afternoon of copious cold Campari Spritzes, long lingering Jacuzzi kissing and multi-partner sex, was underway.

"You never know your luck in a big city" is an old saying that rings true, and that day was beyond any luck that any two young guys should ever expect to receive.

As it happened they were sisters from a wealthy family and therefore had a lavish apartment that wasn't usually normal for a twenty-one-year-old and a twenty-three-year-old.

As soon as the drinks were poured the suggestion was "let's drink these babies in the spa". With clothes off, it was into the Jacuzzi. There I got my first view of the girls - and the apartment. This was quality-class all the way. The two boys had chosen VERY well. Andrew's Best Friend was as eager as I was to be used and abused, but the heat kept us just idling along in semi-erect states for the time being.

Andrew and Elena were already in the spa when suddenly I was dipped head-first into the cold, rose-colored delights of Claudia's Spritz. The cold hit me instantly and I slightly recoiled with the shock. I shouldn't have worried, as Claudia's warm mouth was quickly engulfing me, like all good cocksuckers do, right to the very base.

MMMmmm - I just relaxed and let her work her magic on

me. She slipped off me, took another sip, held it in her mouth and descended on to me again. This time the cool liquid encapsulated my whole shaft in its delectability. With a few more tongue laps of my length, she withdrew, taking Jason's hand and leading him to the bubbling waters.

Wheeee! In I went, deep into the bubbling foam. If you've ever watched clothes being tossed around in a washing machine, then you'll get some idea of what we appendages have to put up with when our bosses decide to subject us to what they call a delightful treat.

Left. Right. Left. Swirl around. Bow down. Point up. More left. More right. It's literally worse than a Drill Sergeant abusing his new intake of raw recruits. And what's more, we penises have no control over the violent action of the currents.

But we weren't totally forgotten amidst all the kissing and drinking and laughter that was happening above the foamy waterline. Hands caressed me and stiffened me. I was stroked and massaged and The Balls were delighted by the tickling and the occasional little nipping.

Jason stood up for a moment and there was a nice "wow" from the two Giovane donna who hadn't seen me before in my glory stance.

"Si. Si. Si! Bellissimo," they said as one, each sending a kiss of approval from their lips via their fingers towards me.

"You are so fortunate Mr. Jason to have such a fine friend" added an envious Elena who had already tied her initial dalliance to be with Andrew but silently knew that by afternoon's end I was going to be had by her too.

"I'll get more drinks," said Claudia - and exited the spa.

Elena indicated Andrew to also stand up. As a deft temptress, she used her hand to bring Andrew's best friend to be nearly face-to-face with me and she began working her tongue in the most magical of ways on the heads of both of us. Plunging into her warm mouth was a relief from all the battering that I'd been taking under water. Oh, yes, this was a Roman luxury I could take a lot of.

"Well, will you look at that. I leave for a minute and my greedy sister makes herself right at home..."

"Do you boys ever fuck each other?" said Claudia without batting an eyelid.

Both Bosses coughed in a loud, embarrassed way before Andrew spluttered out "NO" in a somewhat startled and defining way.

"What makes you ask that?" added Andrew.

"Oh, nothing really.... Just the easy rapport that you both have about being naked with each other. That's really nice to see as so many guys can't cope with that. Elena and I, though we're sisters, both enjoy giving pleasure to each other and to other women - as well as to men" she quickly added.

"You're ... you're... lesbian" stammered Andrew.

"Just sometimes. We like variety in our sex" added Claudia.

"But today, my boys, we are all yours..."

With the initial revelation of woman-on-woman sex, Jason had sent a forceful message of interest directly to me. Up to this time in our lives, we hadn't actually had the opportunity of witnessing live, girl-on-girl action, but I knew from the magazines and porn sites Jason viewed that this was a taboo subject that would always push him into new and stimulating territory. I was soon standing hard-as-a-rock erect whereas it didn't seem to have the same interest to Andrew, as his Best Friend was soon hanging limply looking directly at the bubbling waters beneath him.

With drinks refreshed and the conversation back on to heterosexual experiences, the afternoon was soon revolving around we two Best Friends sitting on the spa edge being sucked. This was followed by me being stroked between two rather large and voluminous breasts while Jason and the others all sniffed a bottle of poppers as it was passed between the four - and then it was into the master bedroom for a delectable foursome.

Through experience I realized that both Andrew and Jason would have no doubt preferred different rooms for their sex because they didn't want to judge each other's performance - but the girls insisted that a foursome should only ever be held in the one room where each party could watch and hear the enjoyment that the others were embracing. So, there was no arguing over that. Personally, I think that Elena was very jealous that she didn't have me as her first choice, so she wanted to check out Claudia's performance so that she could give Jason and I a better one later in the day.

I knew that I was going to enjoy the afternoon and the bedroom sex began with Andrew and Elena playing on the bed, whereas Jason and I began with a long standing-up kissing session with Claudia. Naturally, as the kissing became more intense, so I was pushed ever-so-gently towards my natural place in the world - her velvet purse. There was a layer of trimmed black bush to slip past before this natural amphitheater opened for me but I was right there gently nudging the direction that Jason also wanted me to go.

I caught glimpses of the other two kissing and then with Elena on her back, Andrew moved down south and began to eat her lesbian style. Of course, he couldn't hear me think that observation but it was a very lesbian action if you cared to think of it that way.

As a result of Andrew's intense tongue actions, it was my first experience of hearing Italian opera sung quietly and sweetly during foreplay by Elena. Even that did not prepare me for hearing it sung so *forte* when I gave Claudia her orgasm but we'll come (so to speak) to that soon.

When hearing the sweet humming and singing of the other two lovebirds, both Jason and Claudia looked their way and decided to join them on the bed where I was immediately plunged into Claudia's mouth. I suspect because Jason thought that all this singing was not what he wanted to hear during sex, that this was a good way to stop a female duet happening anytime soon.

Andrew looked up from his tongue exploration and decided to do the same. So, with a quick movement he straddled Elena's head and in went his now nearly erect Best Friend. I could soon hear Andrew's moans as my counterpart was pushed to full erection. Both girls were on their back and both had hot young man sausage in their mouth. That meant both guys were on their knees side by side. With a wicked glint in her eye, Claudia indicated to Jason "Give him a kiss".

Now, The Boss is always up for a good time and always willing to push a boundary or two, so he did. With a firm hand behind Andrew's head, he brought his travel buddy's head to his own lips - and kissed him - passionately. Andrew was amazed, and his eyes popped wide-open in surprise, but the grip was too tight and he was held firmly against Jason's enthusiastic lips.

Both girls nearly choked in surprise. How both of us Best Friends didn't get a tooth mark I just don't know! But we surely gagged them both as they automatically reacted by pushing forward their head in surprise. All I saw was her startled gag reflex tighten before her head once again fell back into the pillow.

As the lips separated, both the guys laughed out loud (or I think that's what I heard while buried deep inside her larynx). I was fully erect, not only from Claudia's efforts but because Jason obviously got turned-on by straying into the VERY taboo territory of kissing his best mate. I learned later that Little Andrew was given the same treatment by Big Boss Andrew – the thrill of forbidden we'll-never-talk-about-this-ever-again-big-brother-type-sex-action surged down the message chain and converted right into hard-as-steel erection power. Watching woman-on-woman action just simply didn't have the same revving power that buddy-bonding kissing seemed to produce. I learned a lot that afternoon about the true feelings and urges that The Boss had kept under wraps all these years. And at that early stage of proceedings I could only wildly imagine what was actually happening within Andrew's well-established masculinity boundaries

- turmoil from brain cells to penis tip I suspected. How wrong that turned out to be – it was also a huge turn-on for Andrew too.

That little bit of action catapulted the sex session into high gear. Not only were the boys now running on high octane adrenalin, so were the two girls. Seeing the two boys kiss had sent a charge of power into their very depths and that hot masculine fire needed urgent extinguishing.

Side by side, the boys added some additional lubrication to their chosen, already very well lubed girl - and in we two penises went. No waiting, and taking no prisoners. And not a condom in sight.

I found that I was very excited by the vacation the boys were having, particularly as I was gaining new insight into the exotica of women from different countries. Unlike back at home where vaginal aromas were much of a muchness, here in Europe I was finding the unique pleasures of slightly different aromas were in some way reflecting on their eating and hygiene habits. On that day, I had the distinct heady scent of Italian cuisine as I moved backward and forwards inside Claudia. I knew from The Boss how much the aroma of different foods attracted his palate or otherwise, and so it was, down here with me. A little fish was always pleasant and sometimes, like at this event, a touch of spice and maybe tomato was adding a wonderful euphoria to my movements. No wonder Andrew had been so engrossed with the delights that Elena had offered his tongue.

With little warning, Andrew was the first to want to shoot.

"Pull out. Pull out" Elena cried, and just in time, as Andrew shot his juice all over her massive breasts.

I was in Claudia, nice and deep. I was rubbing against her engorged mountain of happiness and as a result, she had begun a little singing as she drifted further and further into her own world of pleasure. She began to grind into the mattress so I knew that I would soon fulfill her fantasies.

Jason sent me the message. He'd already seen his mate shoot copiously all over the other sister but he was determined for me to stay inside and give her total pleasure from the full load he intended pumping into her.

With several full thrusts, I was in deeper than Claudia had hoped for. And as I prepared to spew forth my contents I angled to give a final pleasure-of-no-return movement to her mountain - and I released my flume. At that same very moment, she hit a high note that echoed triumphantly around the room and the whole apartment. It was a grand operatic orgasm that told the world "Fuck You" in no uncertain terms. I pulsed and pulsed and pulsed inside her. From the depths, I could hear the cheers from the other team. It had a been a good afternoon for everyone.

In Rome in summer, no-one except the tourists eats before eleven in the evening - it's simply too hot. So, with a shower, a wine and another spa the early evening continued for the four of us. Yes, the girls did put on a small show for the boys and both Jason and Andrew were intrigued. That display got me really aroused. Jason was so intrigued to be so close to watch the action that he sent a constant string of messages down to me. Seemingly every tongue movement was a tantalizing additional notch in his ever-increasing horniness.

When the girls had finished, Elena was very turned-on

and because she hadn't orgasmed that afternoon, she desperately wanted Jason and me to do that for her. So, while Andrew and Claudia enjoyed the spa we returned to the bedroom to give Elena her orgasm. She was very pleased with my big head and girth stimulating her nerve ends and had no intention of me pulling out before I also creamed inside her.

After that, it was time for a meal and a walk to the nearby Trevi Fountain. How Jason and I fell into the shallow water when he threw the coin over his shoulder is anybody's guess, but perhaps it was a combination of the heat, the wine talking and the resulting unsteadiness on his feet. There was much laughter from the ever-present crowd, anger from the police and not to mention my own embarrassment when the shorts fell off and I was exposed to what seemed like a thousand cameras. I was now a celebrity exposed to a waiting world. But as someone famous once said, it pays to advertise.

As a result, that night and most of the next day we spent in the beds of two Australian girls who were hitchhiking their way around Europe - all because they liked what they saw as Jason stood semi-naked in the cool water. I was definitely Jason's good luck charm, his "carrot" for dangling in front of potential playmates. In this instance, it worked a treat, for even though I was only in a state of semi-erection, looking down into the money-littered base of the fountain and then at the coin-throwing throngs, the late afternoon shafts of light caught my wet hardness highlighting it for all to see and admire.

As Kylie and Ashley helped us out of the water it was obvious that Jason and I (and Andrew) were prime meat for the taking. Consequently, as soon as we could, we "lost" Claudia and Elena in the throning crowds and continued on with the two Aussie girls. The day was far from over and it was going to be a busy night for me, and for Andrew's Best Friend too.

Here's to La Dolce Vita - the Good Life!

AMSTERDAM
"Awe. Aaargh! EEEeeeehh!"

Being tucked under as Jason rode the ancient black bicycle on the cobblestones of old Amsterdam was not what I would call easy or joyful. In fact, it was downright painful and bruising. Even The Balls complained about every stone and bump he lurched us over. There was no padding at all on the bike's seat - just the most basic of a practical HARD iconic-shaped saddle, with a shaft of hardness pointing in the direction we were heading and two depressions for a bit of butt to settle into.

No wonder it wasn't long before The Butt Boys decided that enough was enough. The Balls and I, here in Jason's front, don't tend to complain very much as we are somewhat tender, and The Boss usually is very quickly reminded that if he wants to reliably call an erection in the near future then he'd better look after us in the meantime. Give us pain or angst, and we'll destroy any evening of potential lust.

"Jeez, I'm sorry honey. But I just can't seem to get it up tonight" is not what any girl wants to hear at the end of a romantic evening. And that's not what Jason wants either, hence our unspoken agreement to act in each other's best interests.

But not so, The Butt Boys. They take a lot to get riled but when they do, we just go along for the ride. It's a bit like having the bully do the work for you.

And that afternoon they were feeling the bruising of every cobblestone. They ached, they twitched from side to side, they groaned annoyance, they were pissed off that they were being ignored. These nasty boys have got great muscle control so when the cry went out that "enough was enough" they pulled the plug by tightening the muscles from sphincter to kneecap. "Give him a cramp" I heard one of The Butt Boys call out. And they did.

It had an INSTANT impact, as we immediately crashed headlong into a flower vendor. All I saw from under the shorts where I was free-balling were scattered tulip bulbs, various wooden clogs with hairy and or stockinged legs in them and someone's upside down ice-cream cone on the cobblestones.

Talk about commotion! The noise was deafening as everyone shouted in a foreign language, each giving their own interpretation of the event and what should be done with this misguided, dangerous tourist disaster riding their genteel streets and bridges.

"Come, my lad. You need a drink to steady you" said a voice in English but with a heavy accent.

Dragging one stiff leg behind him, my "walking-wounded" Jason made his way to the coffee shop.

"You need a cake with coffee" insisted the man. "One of the specials, please."

Being new to the city, Jason was unaware of the difference between the coffee shops of Amsterdam. One sold coffee and cakes that your grandmother could enjoy, the other sold "special" cakes - which had ye good olde hashish (or marijuana) included in them.

Now, we down here in nether land, didn't know this either, so when we heard Jason order a second "special" cake "because it tasted so good" we naturally thought that he was recovering from his fall and that we'd soon be on our way to the Red-Light District just over another canal or two.

By the time Jason was ready to leave, he was a giggling mess. The Butt Boys had by now released the cramping and Jason was, shall we say, a wee bit disorientated and unsteady on his feet.

"I live just over the road with my sisters," said the new friend. "Come, I'll take you to meet them. Don't worry about the bike, we'll come back for it later."

We crossed the road, went along a side laneway and entered a very narrow building (but then, aren't they all in old Amsterdam).

"Jenny, Agnita - are either of you free? We have a visitor who needs some attention."

Well, how were we to know that it was a brothel and it was going to be ME that was going to get all the attention?

"In here, me darlin'," said the friendly female voice.

"You're in good hands now son, so I'll leave you to it. Enjoy little Jenny's delights. I'll just take the payment from your wallet so you don't have to worry about it."

Jason just purred along with all this, lying on his back, laughing, totally off-his-head, in another world from the effect of eating the cakes. It wasn't long before I was exposed to a dark, heavily curtained bedroom, looking up at a single lightbulb in the ceiling and with umm, shall we be kind and say a mature, going on middle-aged woman of considerable abilities and experience in the sexual pleasuring industry, gazing directly at me.

"My, my what a delightful LITTLE friend you have there," she said, looking at me a little disappointingly.

"LITTLE!!!! LITTLE!!!!" I indignantly wanted to respond. I'd heard of the God-given gifts that many a Dutchman has been provided with and, over the previous few nights, I'd seen a couple of naked Dutchmen that proved the theory once and for all. Perhaps I was of mere "average" size compared to the local men, but in my eyes, back home I was regarded as a dipstick of the most desirable size.

"I'll have to iron out that limpness with my mouth and tongue..." she continued. And then all I saw was darkness.

"Herrings with onions" was all I could think of when her breath enveloped me. My visit must have interrupted her late lunch. And not a fresh mint lozenge to be smelt anywhere.

I was right about her oral skill set. Ok, she started with the old up and down, tried and true, exercise regime and that got me moving towards a semi-erection, but it was the drizzled honey that sent me rocketing to a full-blown, granite strength man-size hard on. And when she licked me and took that golden nectar into her mouth slurp by slurp, lap by lap, I was hers, to be done with in any way she wanted. Jason felt the same. His laughter was now replaced by lots of "oohing" and "ahhing" and grinding his naked body into the fabric of the bed. He was totally unaware of where he was or the age of the woman doing the pleasuring - he just wanted it to never cease.

"Ve fucks now," said Madame Jenny. "You have paid the bareback price, so I lubes your little pricky and in he goes...."

"H-E-L-L-O in there," I shouted to the Tunnel of Love - and all I got back was an echo. I was inside Cavity Central. I'd never seen so much empty space in one woman before. Even with the size that I am and being erect to my full capacity, I couldn't rub anywhere near the sides.

I WAS PLUNGING INTO A DEEP, NOTHINGNESS VOID!!!!!

As the movements continued all I heard was more of Jason giggling and "oohing" and "ahhing" and Jenny shouting "Vuck me, boy. I vide you like a vucking horse..."

It was then that I noticed that there was a certain lining on one wall of the chamber that looked distinctly like a mold - a something that one just instinctively knew was not in my best interests should I rub up against it.

Well, I *was* being ridden by a jockey with the winning post in sight. She was queening me but facing Jason's feet as she rode (obviously being mean I suggest she did that as she didn't want Jason to see who was fucking him). From my point-of-view, I was being thrust in ultra-deep - and at angles the old in-out method just wouldn't reach. Yep, the moldy wall was coming right for my head.

SPLOSH - straight into the bacteria, deep into my eye

and along the side of my head.

"Jeez that stings in my mouth" I responded to myself. But I wasn't close enough to cumming to swill it out with my vomit for there were no messages transmitting from The Boss's addled brain about wanting me to prepare to shoot. He was in another dimension, enjoying every thrust and withdraw that Jenny's jockeying gave him and therefore couldn't care less about my health dilemma. He was totally oblivious to the internal time-bomb that was now ticking in and around me.

Up went Jenny before sliding back down again on me. This time I was thrust to the clean side. Up again she went, only this time she returned and clenched her muscles tightly around me.

"Ok guys" I shouted to The Balls. "This one we have to do ourselves. The Boss is not responding and I need a quick flushing out before I totally swallow a nasty and we're put out of business for a week or more."

Well, it doesn't happen often, but sometimes in the heat of the moment, messages can get mixed, garbled, and words can be misinterpreted. And that was one of those times.

"Flushing out" was taken by The Balls and their higher command as "pissing out" - and that's what I did. Not voluntarily, mind you, but it happened, and there's no denying that.

I saw that single room light so quickly it would make your head spin.

"Vat the vuck you doing.... you're pissing in me, all over me - you little turd."

She was off the bed in a flash, desperately reaching for a towel to wipe herself and to throw one over the continuous cascade of last night's beer-fest re-entering the world before it soaked her bedding and tools of employment.

"Get out! Get out!" she screamed, while I sent urgent messages to The Boss to stem the flow. The towel descended on me, thus cutting off my view of the proceedings.

As my flow ceased I was unceremoniously pushed into the loose-fitting shorts, and I held on for the rough ride as Jason was bodily pushed down the narrow stairs by the man who had brought us to meet his sister. This "family" was not at all what Jason and I had imagined when being picked up from the remains of the flower stall.

Into the street we were flung and with a loud bang, the heavy door was closed behind us.

And dear reader, do I suspect that you want to know whether or not I survived my bout with the bacterial wall?

Well - a few days later I was indeed a very sick penis. "Like pissing razor blades" was the anguished cry I heard from up above.

"AAAARRRRKKKKKKKK!!!!!!!!!!!! And as for the rash on the side of my head, let's just say, it wasn't pretty.

The Butt Boys felt the end of a very long needle whereas I just had this rough, raspy throat condition for a few days that gave Jason all those razor moments. Sweet tasting medicinal juices soon soothed that as they flowed through my insides and out to the bowl. The combination of the two soon had me fit and clean and ready to meet more new friends. But that had to be back home as my little STI escapade - (that's Sexually Transmitted Infection as the young blond Scandinavian nurse explained) - put an end to the last few days of the vacation as far as sex was concerned. Not even a wank - it was too painful.

Of course, this left the game wide open for Andrew to keep bedding the girls and to eagerly pass our lead on the Pussy Scoresheet. And if memory serves me right, the final score that was tallied as they waited to board the plane home was -

Andrew - 37
Jason (read: ME) – 32

It was one of the very few times that I have lost a challenge of this kind.

As the two good friends clinked the beer glasses to celebrate Andrew's victory you could almost hear the audible sigh of relief from the European girls that we were finally on the plane home – at least, that was what Jason's ultra-large ego imagined. With the new day, we arrived home with two new phone numbers in Jason's pocket. It was looking like business as usual, but...

******

It was about a week after we got home from the European trip and I was fully recovered from the Bacteria Battles when the itching and the scratching began in earnest.

After a few days, I could feel the patter of what seemed like a thousand little feet at the pubic hairline and more distantly, deep within the re-grown pubic hair forest. Occasionally, also along the hairs on the sac.

It was a shock to realize that I WAS NOT ALONE!

It was more like a tickle, a bit like what it would feel if a long caterpillar with all its myriad of legs and feeler hairs moved itself slowly along the back of your hand – a slightly creepy feeling that your body was being invaded by stealth.

There was nothing that either I or The Balls could do about it. We were just the lunar landscape and they were the exploring scientists - creeping, crawling and egg-laying as they went.

The Boss scratched the occasional itch but thought nothing more of it until that fateful telephone call...

"YOU'VE GIVEN ME CRABS!!!" the hysterical female voice shouted down the phone to the answering machine. "I'm diseased from you and your European trollops. God knows where your pubes, let alone your dick has been dipping its wick or rolling in the hay. Fuckin' hell Jason, it feels like my pubes are alive and dancing The Macarena Scratch and Itch. I feel so damn dirty I could cry. Fuck off, you diseased man-whore. I don't ever want to see you again." Click.

Jason responded to the recorded message with a bewildered "What the ...." and quickly dropped his trousers and boxers to begin his own crime scene investigation at the site of the alleged insurgents.

Within his thick black growth just north of where I hung, he couldn't immediately see anything worrying, so we moved across to under a redirected desk lamp in order to put more light on the situation.

The pubes were now bathed under an intense spotlight - and no doubting it, there they were. The dark blobs against the white skin, sitting there like black freckles. He jumped up, totally amazed at the discovery. It was as if he saw something about himself that he'd never seen before. We entered the bathroom to get the tweezers. Just to convince himself that these were living, biting, egg-laying vermin, he then plucked one off his pubes and placed it on the white porcelain hand basin. Bent over the specimen and with the strong shaving light turned on to spotlight it, he was like a modern-day medical laboratory scientist watching and waiting for something to grow or move in a Petri dish. He repeated the exercise with a plucked hair or two that had a little egg firmly attached to it.

I could see him bending down really close in eager anticipation. And as for me, I was relieved that at least one of the noisy little critters was no longer annoying me with its multitudinous legs doing military precision marching routines.

"Awe fuck... did you see that. It moved" And bent down even closer to watch the legs continue to move and prove to himself, that it really was alive and capable of movement.

"I'VE GOT CRABS" shouted a now near hysterical Jason to Jerry down the phone, thus repeating, even more dramatically, the hysteria he'd heard for himself only a few minutes before.

"What do I do...?"

"Man, it's no big deal. Just go to the drugstore and get some cream, smear it on all over you, leave it for ten minutes, wash off and you're a hundred percent ok again. And, oh yes, you gotta wash all the clothes you've been wearing, all the towels as well as the sheets just in case there are some eggs or live ones still there lying in wait."

"I will. I will. Absolutely. A hundred percent..." he stammered back, totally paranoid that such little creatures could have had such a devastating effect on his sex life.

Well, let me tell you, I've never before (or I suspect since) seen The Boss so industrious. On arriving back from the drugstore, it was everything off, and I do mean everything. The pile of clothing, sheets, towels, jocks, cum towels and more became a mountain of industrial proportions. No item that had contact with his body in the last week or so escaped the hot wash cycle. The washing machine went non-stop that night and again into the next day. If his mother had arrived at the apartment during this cleansing cycle she would have been suitably impressed to know that her son wasn't the water-avoiding, hygiene-hating bum that she had for so long believed that he was.

But by jeez, the smell and taste of that crab-destroying cream was seemingly also of industrial toxicity and stench. If that old adage about things only being good for you if they taste or smell bad is true, then there were absolutely no problems with Jason and I being purity itself after this cleansing exercise.

SLOSHHHH!!!!!!! A handful of cream was slapped across my shaft, massaged deeply all over The Balls with heaps more to follow in the pubic forest area. It was cold and thick and gooey and felt like what I suspect a jello wrestler would feel like – without the unpleasant smell, of course. Oh, yes, that smell... At least I had only the one outlet where I could detect it, and it certainly caused me to become a shrinking violet as a result of it. There would be no sex in the immediate future until I returned to a normal state of cleanliness.

Jason was fastidious about applying the cream to EVERYWHERE on his body and head! And not just the once. I was just getting used to the drying effect the cream was having on my shaft when another splosh "just for good measure" was heaped upon me and my surroundings. The clock was set for ten minutes and while we waited, out came the fine-tooth comb that was supplied with the lotion that would be used to discover any more eggs on the hairs after our shower. Also, the scissors. Obviously, at least a trim would be in order, perhaps even a total pubic makeover with waxing or shaving. Jason was so off the planet with disgust that goodness knows what was going through his mind as to how to avoid this catastrophe in the future.

In my view, the end of the ten minutes couldn't come quick enough. It felt like that I could feel every one of the now stiff, dry hairs. My crumpled shaft was like an arid desert mud-pool baking dry in the hot sun. The smell was like Essence of Auto Exhaust and it kept me totally limp and sexless.

"Jee-zus, Jason, let's get this showering session underway..." I tweaked up to him.

It seemed like that it could have easily been a nominee for the longest shower in history. How many times can hair be shampooed, washed, body-lotioned, combed, rubbed, inspected, scratched? Well, it seems – excessively. The fact that he started drying off with a contaminated towel used that morning didn't help in the shortening of that process. Fortunately, he'd only begun drying his arms before realizing his gigantic oversight of not replacing the towel with a new one. So, it was back under the shower for yet another additional scrub. I tell you, I have never felt so clean in all my days of hanging around with Jason. And what a relief to get rid of most of the smell. But Jason, Jason, Jason – did we really need all of that tin of powder PLUS the after-shave to try and disguise the remnants of the odor! I smelt like an escapee from a perfume factory after having trialed an indulgence of samples.

He did find an additional egg or two on the hairs and these, along with the now dead carcasses of the crabs, he displayed triumphantly on a sheet of pure white office paper. Like a commanding general leading his foot-soldiers, he had bravely and very manly, fought and overcome the wicked crab foe that he himself had imported from Europe. Now with a clean slate and much the wiser, he was ready to again move forward seeking new female frontiers to conquer and enjoy.

Later that night he pondered one of the great philosophical sexual questions of our times – would he begin shaving those pubes again in order to stop a possible repeat invasion or could he contemplate the thought of having another extraordinarily painful waxing?

By the next morning, the deeply etched memories of the previous tortuous waxing event had flooded back to him. He surmised that there was really no desire on his part to be tortured like that often – or even, ever again. So, it was no surprise when he looked down at me and said

"Buddy, you know what – we'll trim!"

I think that we were both pleased with that decision (well, at least for the foreseeable future).

I tweeted back my approval for it was nice for the both of us to be back to normal once more – two horny studs, the very best of friends, out looking for a good time.

Bring it on!!!!!

*Why is it that lovers help each other undress before sex,
yet after sex, always dress on their own?*

PETER BENN

CHAPTER FIVE

THE DEVIANT AND SINNERS SWINGERS GROUP

Like most of what Jason does, he took the challenge when it was presented to him. Pique his curiosity about interesting sex, and he's yours to do with, whatever that might involve.

The "lots of women, all naked, all up for it" comment was all that it took for us to be on our way to outer suburbia one Saturday night. We were heading for a swingers group that one of Jason's friends had attended. This was one of their "open nights" which allows a few additional single males to attend without throwing the male/female ratio too off-center. For Jason, this was ideal, as it would allow him to be as slutty as he liked without any jealous repercussions from an attached girlfriend. I know that he can also be jealous, so watching a girlfriend having sex with other men might just be all too much for him to cope with too. But tonight, he was a free agent and was looking forward to a fun time.

The house was situated in some woodland off a major road, therefore being private to only those who were invitees. The website said that it was very spacious with an 8-person spa, a pool, huge entertaining area with a bar, change rooms and four private rooms as well as three communal play areas complete with beds, additional mattresses, and bathrooms. On arrival, guests were encouraged to slip into something erotic for the mingling, get-to-know-you, aspect of the party. Exotic underwear, leather, something outrageous - all good to get the mind and the libido focused.

We changed in the first change-room into a pair of backless jocks. He was happy to show off his hairy but trimmed buttocks as he knew that they would attract attention. The front pouch was stretchy so that I'd firstly, have a comfortable front-row position to show off my slack at-ease size, and secondly, as the eroticism kicked in, I could grow to my full length and make a more positive impression. Jason and I both knew that the jocks wouldn't be on for long so it was just to fit into the protocol of the early part of the evening.

What was a bit unusual for my master was that he seemed to be suffering that night, from a touch of Pre-Performance Anxiety Syndrome. The bravado of the self-styled "chick magnet" wasn't kicking-in early in the evening's procedure. He was there without the support of his buddies who used each other to incite greater daring and sexual exploits. For a while, it looked like I might unexpectedly remain in that pouch for some considerable time.

Walking into the entertainment room, already filling with other eager couples, a few single women and a number of competing single guys, he made a bee-line for the bar. He needed some alcohol fuel to get him feeling more comfortable and help the loosening of his inhibitions. From what I could see through the stretched fabric of the pouch there were going to be many opportunities for a fun night - though perhaps with a much older mature crowd than he was used to. In his haste to get to a swingers group, perhaps he'd overlooked the fact that he was young - and in some cases, he was VERY young meat, compared to those he was surveying across the room. This wasn't an event to attend unless you were happy to have mature-aged women lust after you so that they could enjoy the physical benefits of young mutton instead of their usual aged beef. Cougars were definitely on the prowl that night.

And perhaps he had also overlooked the fact that swinger parties also cater for the bi-lady and gentleman who liked to take the occasion to play with the same sex. Some bisexual mature-age men also like young male stud-muffins to enjoy to the full, this being such a change from their usual mature female sexual companions.

So, it should have been no surprise when the silver-haired gent and his attractive older female companion started a conversation. Backed into a corner by the two, Jason had no escape. The woman's breasts were very attractive and because of the coolness of that part of the room, stood erect and pointed straight at my man.

"Well, hello gorgeous" was her opening remark, as she raised a hand and rubbed it gently across Jason's pecs. "Welcome to our little group of deviants and sinners. We trust that you will have a wonderful night. I'm Marge and this pervert is my husband John."

"I'll second that," said John, as he reached to give what Jason thought was going to be a handshake, but instead was a warm friendly squeeze of my position within the pouch.

Jason jumped in surprise but I was ok with that. ANYONE who takes an interest in me is always welcome. "Fondle me, squeeze me, suck me - just don't ignore me" - is my motto. And with the squeeze, he gave me an added tweak just to be sure that I'd send a message up to Jason that he was interested in a man-on-man session later on.

"WHOA" spat out Jason having got the intended message. "I'm not gay you know!"

"No-one said you were" gently replied the man. "That's just a friendly "hello" at a place like this.... but if you *are* interested, you know that I am too."

Jason certainly now knew that he wasn't in Kansas anymore and that the night was only going to get more confusing as it went along.

We made our excuses and drifted across the room to join a group of three younger women. This was more what Jason was looking for and it wasn't long before the alcohol began to kick in and all four were talking the talk. Each of the women dressed differently, including two, being bare-breasted with seductively little panties, the third was happily already totally naked. All three of them displayed ink somewhere on their body.

"So you're a swinging virgin" the naked one jokingly enquired of Jason. "Well, we'll have to fix that won't we girls" she added, as she winked at them in a manner that suggested they all go and find a room immediately.

She took control and kissed my man. I was immediately jolted into action by an urgent message from him. And when the other two women started on his nipples and then stroked my growing size in an amorous and suggestive way, it was definitely "off to a room" without delay. When another warm feminine hand slipped into the rear opening of his jocks and began to stroke his buns, a four-way was assured.

Into a bedroom, we went. The hosts were very generous in their approach to making everyone feel right at home. This particular room had a generous king size bed, lots of pillows, supplies of condoms, poppers, lubricant, towels and subdued romantic lighting. I knew this because by the time we reached the room I had been released from Jason's jocks and I had an upstanding view of Jason's new friends.

Without the need for discussion, the three women subdivided a part of Jason's body as their own and began the enjoyment of working on him for both their, and his, pleasure. The original naked girl (they were all naked now), continued her kissing, another worked her tongue on his nipples, while the third, when she saw me, purred enthusiastically...

"Mmmm big boy - that's a nice size for me to play with."

Now, with attention like that, I'm not going to disappoint. After a quick view of the room, I was suddenly engulfed in darkness by a pair of decadently painted red lips attached to a very agile mouth that descended on to me, all glossy and wet. There was no doubt that there would be evidence left on his groin from when she totally deep

105

throated me - a red-lipped calling card silently telling the next deep-throat exponent that she had a reputation to live up to. In the meantime, she was certainly up to the job of making me a happy, horny "woman's best friend".

Being so well-looked after by no less than three women, Jason was in seventh heaven. Just wait until he shares this with his mates in the bar. The number will escalate to be at least five horny women, they will all be tempestuous, horny beauty queens starved of affection from young men like him and they will all - repeatedly - keep coming back for more, more, more! As you know, bar stories only ever have a small grain of truth in them and the constant retelling of tonight's sexual conquest saga will be no exception – but we already know that about Jason, don't we!

Through my brief appearances back into the room, I could see that we had attracted an audience. With our open-door policy, other horny men and women came and went, our activities stimulating their growing libidos. One man fondled the ass of one of the girls, but Jason was quick to move him on with a "fuck off" flick of his hand. Jason had no intention of willingly sharing his sexual banquet with anyone else.

Oh, I did so love the way I was treated by my new Oral Momma. Some women are blessed with a tongue that may cut a rival to the quick with sharp words, but when they use that same mouth for Sausage Service as I could call it, I can but remain upright and let them have their wicked ways with me. This brilliant practitioner of the finer art of masculine pleasuring was no doubt not only an outstanding graduate of Oral College but an Honors Graduate into the bargain. What couldn't this experienced young woman do....

"Choke the Chicken" - she nimbly slipped her mouth along my length, right to my roots

"Lick the Dick" – self-explanatory

"Gaga Gagging" - my head enjoyed her agile attempts to let me see down her windpipe, dark that it was

"The Butterfly Flick" - Whoa! - such a nimble tongue flick and spot-on for my F-spot (that's my super-sensitive frenulum skin just under my head. If you don't know it and use it, then time to wise-up and get knowledgeable, adding it to your arsenal of tricks in order to give your guy the best possible blow-job)

and not forgetting...

"The Vacuum" - take it from me, the one who knows these things most intimately, it's the BEST feeling ever and oh, so, guaranteed to get me over-excited and spewing my storage tanks. As I say to anyone who wants to be best friends with a penis - "Just cover me with your mouth, suck out the air and ride me like a champion rodeo rider". It's ooh, so oh, so fuckin' fantastic."

And don't be surprised to hear me shout "Do it again. Do it again!!!" as I lose control and just let it all happen, as indeed it is guaranteed to do. Ye oldie vacuum technique will also get you a much larger volume of my juice than you might have otherwise been expecting. Just warning like ... as I don't want you to get all spewy and spluttery as you try to swallow the additional load and then take it out on Jason for not warning you that he was even close, let alone had a half a gallon of man juice stored inside that needed an urgent exit valve.

Yep - this girl was really experienced in knowing how to handle me and excite me. Upstairs loved it too though he was also a touch busy with the other two ladies. Still, I kept receiving the "Good job. Keep it going - but shit – DON'T SHOOT YET. I want to fuck at least one of these beauties" messages from him. I could feel the excitement coursing through him as the stimulation of both nipple-side and mouth-side kept mounting. I wasn't helping the situation as I was sending him more and more urgent messages along the lines of "I can't hold on too much longer. What am I to do?"

He finally responded to my front-line dispatches and made an attempt to extricate himself from the three passion-pushers.

"Who wants to ride me first" he arrogantly said to the trio, as he deftly showed my hardness and length off to the two girls who hadn't been concentrating in my area. "Jason Junior here is ready for his fun."

"Oral Coral", as I had secretly re-named the girl with the fabulous mouth, decided that she was more interested in lavishing her not inconsiderable oral skills on the hubby and wife team who had unbeknown to me, been using their fingers to considerable advantage on her all the while she was seemingly only concentrating on me. No wonder she moaned and groaned and expressed great feelings upon me. They departed for another location, fingers up crevices and lips longing for labia.

As for me, I was now pointing ceiling-ward awaiting my fate. Would it be Miss A or Miss B I wondered?

"Go for it, bro. Have 'em both" the masculine voice happily chirped in as he stood beside the bed playing with his member, a member who was not nearly as erect as I was – or as big. Of course, watching Jason and myself in action could help rectify that semi-floppy situation.

Before I knew what was what, it was Showtime. Miss A straddled Jason's hips and with one fluid movement descended directly on to me. Wow - no time to sheath me up or add lube to my outside. This girl was already self-lubed and ready for me.

I was immediately plunged into the warm darkness right up to my root base. I hadn't been doing anything except sitting there upright, looking up at the ceiling via her freshly shaved pubes and tight breasts - and her beautiful face that had the wicked smile of a Tatar Conqueror. She had her first conquest for the night and she was going to enjoy it - her wicked, yet delightful smile knew that *she* was in charge and intended to ride me like the marauding female warrior she was.

In between the plunges, I glanced across at The Boss and he was loving every minute of having someone else do the work. It was then that Miss B straddled his face giving him an opportunity to enjoy one of his favorite go-to positions - and a good tongue workout to boot. Jason was being used and abused and he knew he was in the right place with the right open-minded women at the right time.

For me, it was all a hot mix of flashing light followed by long dark explorations of deep internal delights. Rubbing myself against her inner walls just added to my enjoyment.

Every time I surfaced I could hear moans of ecstasy from the whole lot of them. Roll. Tickle. Lick. Vibrate. His tongue never seemed to stop. EVERYONE was having a good time including ME.

But it wasn't going to last!

Without warning, Jason delivered a message to me like a bolt of lightning. Fuck, it caught me totally by surprise!

I was unable to hold back and I convulsed deep within the flesh mines, over and over again. It was so unexpected that I seemed to have no control over my shaft or The Balls. It was as if some external probe had sent a barb to me that pushed me over the edge without warning. Buried deep as I was, how was I to know what had happened up above in the real world. It was only when I saw room light again that I could see the kerfuffle that was going on.

"Shit - give me a towel. NOW - for fuck's sake. Oh, shit! You... you... pissed in my mouth. Fuckin' hell woman. What do you think you were doing?"

Watersports were certainly on Jason's sexual agenda, but obviously, this waterfall arrived a little bit unexpectedly. As he gagged and shouted and swore at all and sundry in the room there was little thought for me as I was thrust from left to right and every other direction as he jumped around the bed cursing and swearing even more.

At that moment, I was just a limp pendulous sausage of no use to man, woman or beast. It was all about HIM - again - as it so often is! Didn't HE just feel the bliss of ME undertaking his bidding and giving Miss A a sticky good time? What of HER coitus interruptus? What about HIM just telling me "what a good willy I am"? What about MY contents now sliding down her leg and in need of wiping? You'd think that a grown man of his age could cope with a bit of sterile water hitting his mouth. If it had been beer, there would be none of this carry-on.

And what of Miss B? Between my violent swings, as I hung there now somewhat limply, I could see that she was very amused by the whole thing.

"I'm a squirter," she said. "It can happen to any girl when she's made excited. Get over it!"

Knowing that the evening between them and Jason was now at a stalemate, the two women decided to take their leave - but not before Miss A bent down to me and gave me a big lipstick kiss right on the top of my head. Obviously well pleased with me, I was chuffed to carry her signature trademark with me (at least until we hit the showers).

"Jeeezus mate, that was a fuckin' horny treat," said the previously silent voyeuring masturbator who now sported a super erection. "Thanks for fluffin' me up" - and with a broad grin, he left.

It was time for a shower and a spa. The night was still young.

Shared showers were simply part of the evening. We had to wait a couple of minutes while others showered but that was no issue. Watching a young man and his lady friend soap each other was a visual delight that certainly piqued the interest of Jason. I was on my way to a good-sized semi-erection by the time they stepped out and began to dry off.

The tactile pleasure that warm water and soap can give is like no other, especially when versatile hands slip and slide into every bodily crevice - and where a hard dick can do the same. Watching others give sensual body pleasure to one another is a horny turn-on for both Jason and myself.

As the warm water flowed down his stomach and on to me I think Jason finally remembered that he, too, had just had pleasure with me. Really, he was always a good master to me, for whenever we had bareback he'd always urinate afterward to clear me out of any possible lurking infections and then soap me all over for the same reason. Invariably I'd thank him for keeping me healthy by growing just a bit harder so that his memory of that good time would last a little longer. Of course, he also gargled and swished out his mouth many more times than necessary in order to remove his inordinate phobia about urine in the mouth. Doesn't he know that's it's totally sterile and pure? Sheeeees-us! But perhaps it's his memory of the incident in the showers with all the other naked guys for the football initiation that still haunts him. That took water-sports to a whole new level.

We found our way back to the bar via a few diversionary investigations into rooms where interesting sounds emanated or where others lingered watching the events taking place inside. The party was now in full swing and it was great to be in a world where exhibiting nakedness and sex were fully accepted by everyone.

"Just look around you - if all the world acted like these party sluts there wouldn't be a need for wars" laughed the middle-aged man sitting opposite.

But for now, we were in the eight-person spa having a relax before our next round of sexual adventures. More precisely, Jason was relaxing and I was swimming, being tossed around in all directions by the somewhat violent jets of water coming from all sides. What with all the bubbles it was a bit hard to focus on what else was

"Down There" in the water with me but I could see at least another half dozen bodies. I could see an overweight woman and her trimmed pussy region, an uncut dick in a high state of arousal, two slender smoothly shaved vaginas and a thick masculine hairy leg that I didn't really care to see what was attached to it.

It's a different world down in the suds to the friendly discussions going on up above. But I have to admit, it's where the real action was happening. There was the male hand actively fingering one of the shaved pussies. Hairy Leg was trying to rub against the rather large naked woman and was being regularly rejected. All myriad of toes seemed to touch and explore, with the occasional foot slipping discretely up the calf giving a more direct "I'm interested. Let's do it" message to the recipient.

When a gentle female hand surreptitiously emerged through the foam and gave me a gentle squeeze, I knew that I had better pay more attention to the messages coming down from The Boss. I was on notice that my second performance for the evening was in the offing.

As I emerged from my bubbly underwater world I could see that he'd picked up a lady of more mature years than is usually his want. But then he does love the occasional more experienced MILF so I knew we'd probably learn a new trick or two tonight to add to his Little Black Book of Pleasure Skills. He has always been good like that. Always willing to experience a woman who is not his normal shagging type just so that the wide spectrum of sexual possibilities can bring him new and often unexpected aspects of pleasuring. Sharon was such a possibility.

As they showered I heard the snippets of conversation about her having had kids and her pussy wasn't as tight as it was before them and as a result, her husband's smallish dick could rarely excite her these days. Jason rattled on about how he adored pleasuring a woman like her because of me and my size he would be able to give her the deep satisfaction and girth she was craving.

As they dried off with the towels, they were joined by a man who was introduced as her husband. From where I hung I could see the truth in her statements about his appendage. I smiled inwardly to myself that I was blessed to be on the largish side rather than playing for the miniature team.

He was going to join us - but only to watch. "And would it be all right to video the event - just for our own private purposes of course," asked Mini Man.

Jason approved, even without asking me. Being photographed was nothing new to us. What seemed like a score of our love-making encounters and sex hookups involved some sort of video or photographic recording. "The Pussy Files" was Jason's name for the folders on his phone and computer that contained his photos and videos displaying me in all manner of positions, bodily parts and states of erection. Add in the swapped photos of his many women, those added to by his buddies and even more downloaded from the internet, and you can imagine it was somewhat bulging with eroticism and blackmail material. Heaven forbid that he ever lost the cell phone or the laptop. Still, I'm happy being a media celebrity of sorts and if anyone else wants to get pleasure from watching what I do, I say "have fucking fun just like I do".

There was one room purely for those who were interested in being photographed. That allowed all the rest of the party attendees to be assured that they were able to retain all the privacy expected from their most intimate moments together.

We weren't alone as we entered that room. It was an orgy room and there were at least ten others in various states of fucking, sucking, kissing, voyeuring and filming. Twosomes, threesomes, and moresomes were on the carpeted floor, the bed, the big armchairs and on the additional mattresses on the floor. As I swiveled around to take in the view, this was a scene that interested me a lot. It was great to see my fellow members hard at work being given pleasure by mouths, pussies, hands and anal sphincters. We penises, as a collective group, were being used and abused - and didn't we love all of it! A party without active dick participation is no fun at all.

As we moved to find a play space we came across a rather handsome middle-aged man who you could say was "just resting" between bouts. He took an immediate liking to our group and to Jason's new-found MILF. Nicely muscled torso, a thick hooded appendage which was already starting to disrobe - and a great smile. No doubt he'd already been a *very* popular addition to the activities in the room. As Jason kissed our Sharon, The Hunk joined in from behind, therefore placing her in a "human sandwich" position between the two of them. Hubby was already filming the action with his cell phone and was delighted that an additional man was now involved. The Hunk spread his large hands across her breasts and pressed his semi-rigid dick upright between her buns so that she would immediately know that he too was interested in her delightful assets.

As they found a comfortable place on a conveniently located mattress on the floor, she lay on her back. Jason moved down her body, licking and tantalizing her with his tongue and lips. Breasts first, then descending ever so slowly to discover the delights of her clit. I knew the instant he had reached The Big C because a message was involuntarily sent to me with a speed and a punch that mimicked lightning. While I was not needed for the moment, I wriggled between Jason's prone crotch and the edge of the mattress. It was all I could do to remind him that carpet burns were possible if he wasn't careful and THAT, my friends, would instantly end a fine evening of frolics followed by several days of sexual incapacity.

He continued to lay on his stomach eating her out. I could hear her moan with ecstasy. My man was very adept at using his tongue to add pleasure - and he was obviously leaving no mini-mountain unturned. When he hummed on her C-spot the cry of orgasm filled the air. I even heard applause from one couple.

By this time The Hunk had dropped to his knees and was feeding her mouth with his large uncut wiener sausage. Hubby just didn't know where to film next. This was beyond his wildest expectations.

Jason kept the messages coming to me and soon I was erect and ready for action. He had prepared his MILF for my arrival not only with his extra-busy tongue but the three-finger lubrication exercise he expertly used. Hubby knew that the action shot was not far off. He could see that I was just the ticket for his wife to enjoy to the hilt. Some balls-deep action captured on video would be exactly what the horny sexually frustrated husband could enjoy over and over again in the privacy of his home office. He was already imagining the magic of his first jack-off session using this footage.

He didn't want more kids, and certainly not as a result of this night's activities, so he unwrapped the condom and handed it to Jason, all the while filming me while the raincoat was gently placed over my head, rolled down my long shaft to protect my sides and lubed some more on the outside. As you can imagine it's difficult enough to see through a condom at the best of times but with that extra lube, the view gets a might blurry.

As Jason deliberately guided me towards her motherlode I still pictured what I saw before I was dressed - pubes as smooth as silk that merged into the fold of the cave-like lips that surrounded her pleasure zone. And there in the middle of this elegant zone, the warm, wet inner lips reached out in their plumpness to welcome the visitor. These were the Lips of Loveliness, the Holy Grail of man's "Search for Paradise". This divine center of femininity had seen her virginity taken, had in earlier days seen her husband's love enacted many times, had seen the birth of her children - and now it was my turn to revitalize her and remind her of how good sex can be with an outsized visiting intruder like myself.

Jason moved forward between her legs until I was neatly positioned between her excited pussy lips. Hubby moved from filming The Hunk being sucked by his wife, down to where Jason was about to live up to his promise of bringing this lady deep orgasmic pleasure. I was as ready as I would ever be – hooded-up, lubed-up, rock hard. I signaled my readiness to Jason and in we went....

Whoa!!!!!!! What a cavern that turned out to be! I am long *and* wide but even I struggled to rub the sides as we moved further in. This woman had done it tough with those kids I thought. No wonder Hubby felt like he was just a small fish in a giant mouth, and couldn't feel a thing.

Still, we moved in and out. We moved sideways and from side to side. We flinched the muscles along my length. We rubbed the clit with every thrust and every withdrawal. Oh, my, that was the part I loved best. My head and her clit were made to bring our master and mistress the greatest of pleasure. Like a puppy that loves to have the back of its neck rubbed, so it is with my head. Press me against her pleasure point and both of us will feel the result, crying out for "MORE, MORE, MORE!"

I was loving all this attention to my head when suddenly I was whipped out into the room light. What was going on?

Our MILF was changing position, as was The Hunk. He had moved onto his back on the mattress, his now very large and very hard dick pointing upwards. After taking a good sniff of poppers handed to her by her still filming husband, our Sharon then lowered herself onto his erection and she began to ride him.

I just stood there still dressed looking directly at both of them going for it.

"SCHLAPP!" Another generous dollop of lube landed on me and Jason started moving me forward. What was going on I asked myself?

Jason's messages were no help other than to say that we're going in. And then it dawned on me...

"FUCKIN' DOUBLE PENETRATION!!!!!!" I screamed in amazement. "WE'RE FUCKIN' SHARING SPACE WITH THE HUNK AND HIS MONSTER DICK."

As a piece of good advice, never, ever, under-estimate

the pliability of the human body when the owner of that body is fired up and in the inferno of sexual combustion.

Even though our MILF was already seemingly chock-a-block with man meat, as Jason and I came knocking on the lower lips we were able to slip in without the slightest resistance. It took only a moment for my head to wriggle under the flaps between her walls and his stiffness. I'll admit that it was a tight fit for the both of us in there and in no way, was The Hunk's Monster going to allow me any additional space. But even so, we both had our cave area to explore and our owners started to co-ordinate their plunges and their retractions. Not only were we giving Mrs. MILF a packed and very full vagina, we were getting and giving pleasures that neither of us as a single dick could achieve. The rubbing of the two of us with each other was something akin to starting a campfire by rubbing two sticks together. It became really intense. As one of us was moved forward, so the other was instructed to back off. And vice versa. Occasionally we'd moved in unison.

And then there was Mrs. MILF doing her own thing as she rode the both of us like a jockey on heat. You would have thought that the coziness of the two of us inside would have satisfied her, but no - in came her finger to add additional self-pleasuring. Would this woman never be satisfied? What, with two dicks AND a fingering of her magic mountain, there was definitely going to be an orgasmic explosion of epic proportions.

Of course, I couldn't see anything being where I was, but I could feel vibrations and muscle twitches and tightening's all around me. EVERYONE was obviously having a fantastic time - including us working furiously in the sex mines down below, at the coalface so to speak.

How long this mutually shared activity was going to last before one of us was going to spill his load was anybody's guess. This shared intimacy was seemingly lasting for ages, varying from hot galloping lust through to a gentle canter by the jockey riding us.

After a while, all the friction between myself and The Monster did start to become a little bit rough on my head and that message I relayed to The Boss. It was time for one of us sausage-heads to withdraw and let the other finish the job unhindered. Jason saw sense and I was gently backed out.

"AAAAwwww – FAAARK" cried an orgasmic Mrs. MILF as I slid out over her vaginal lips, thus giving her some respite from the double-trouble-stretching she'd been (happily) enduring.

My latex covering was whipped off and my head was immediately moved to her mouth. Jason stood astride the reclining Hunk with me at the perfect level for her to suck me while she continued to ride him to climax.

She knew, and Jason knew, and The Hunk knew, that it was rapidly heading towards fireworks time. The Big Bang. The Cum Explosion.

As Jason quickened his pace of thrusting me in and out of her mouth, so The Hunk started riding her, his hips rising from the mattress with each quickening thrust. Mrs. MILF continued unabated with her mouth-filled lustful thrusts along my shaft as well as the up and down piston action of The Hunk deep inside her. Secretly, she no doubt wondered who was going to fill her first.

As it turned out, it was me. I sent the message that I couldn't hold out any longer - and Jason agreed. Spasm after spasm of my juice filled her mouth to such an extent that she was unable to hold it all in. It oozed in sticky streams from the corners of her mouth, then down, like tentacles, on to her neck and breasts. Jason pulled me from her mouth and pointed me downwards - and even more fresh juice spilled from my depths onto those breasts.

Then with one last thrust from The Hunk, he too was over the top, spasming his juices into the condom in her cavernous depths. The Divine Mrs. MILF didn't let that cumming stop her from riding the whole way to the finish line. With dogged determination, she rode him until he shouted for "mercy" with a "fuck you woman. Stop. Stop. S-T-O-P" cry that could be heard across the room and out into the corridor. She had had her way with both men and was totally ecstatic, giving one last orgasmic moan that nearly equaled in volume that of her big boy penetrators.

Hubby was thrilled with the outcome of this unexpected consequence of their dalliance at the swinger's party. The video images he now held in his phone would help fuel his sexual appetite over the long cold winter ahead. Perhaps too, he imagined that his satisfied wife might now make more allowances for him to have sex with her - or so he hopefully dreamed.

"No way, Jose" I was thinking. "She wants and needs only super-size dick from now on. Forget it, man, you're no longer in the race..."

They all fell into a tangle of hot cum and perspiration-soaked bodies, all agreeing that is was some of the best sex that any of them had had in a long while.

And I had to agree. Right now, though, I needed another

hot shower and a good soaking in the spa before our trip home. I also sent Jason a message that there wouldn't be any more sex tonight if it involved me coughing up. I was a bit too sore in the head and needed a rest.

I needn't have bothered, as by mid-morning, when waking and remembering back on the night before, HE decided that he needed a wank, just to start the day. And as he nestled back into the pillows and described on the phone the events of the previous night to one of his friends, I was upright and again being massaged to climax. It was going to be just another day in Jason's world.

When a woman is pregnant, all her friend's touch her stomach and say, "Congratulations".

Why is it that no-one comes up to the husband, touches his penis and says, "Good job".

PETER BENN

CHAPTER SIX

THE BRIDESMAID

"Yeah, bro. Love to. What date again?"
And so, it was settled. Andrew had officially asked Jason and myself - (well technically speaking, only Jason, but where he goes then I'm right there as his right-hand man, wingman, so to speak) - to be one of his best men at his upcoming marriage to Michelle.

This was a big deal between the group of friends that Jason spent much of his guy-time with. On previous drunken nights, they'd discussed the importance of buddies looking after buddies and that they'd all be there for the others when the time was needed. Whether that was during some personal disaster or as each of them married, it didn't matter. Buddies were buddies, and there were no secrets about who needed help, who was getting the most sex and probably most importantly, who was up whom in regard to their women.

"Two bridesmaids - Julie-Ann who you know is her best friend, and then there's Tara. She'll be flying in just for the wedding."

Jason and I had already bedded Julie-Ann more than once. She was a lot like a friend with benefits. If Jason needed a glamorous woman on his arm for a social function at the theater or the office, then she'd often step in and be his date. There were no expectations of romance or a life together, rather, just a friendship where they both enjoyed each other's company for a few hours - and naturally followed by a "thank you" happy ending. We ALWAYS ended up having sex together though not always at home in J-A's bed and not always waiting until after the event we were attending.

Julie-Ann was an adventurous friend, so I was flashed out and put to work in the most unusual of locations. Favorites for me have included the walk-in storage room of the five-star hotel's linen service, in the women's bathroom of the prestigious golf course clubhouse during the trophy speeches - and as a star turn in the backroom of the Fashion Week dressing room where we played to a small but very encouraging, all-male audience who sprang us just as I was being lined up and tunnel bound. She loved her sex raw and had an uncanny ability to self-lubricate just at the mere thought of public sex possibly being on the agenda. Jason and I know no-one else who is so daring or sexually hungry.

There was, of course, that memorable night in the hotel gardens somewhere between the car park and the main lobby where I was whipped out, rock hard, in readiness to press home Jason's hot desire. When I appeared into the open he already had her backed up against a wall behind a very bushy shrub, her dress pulled up, her panties down around her knees and passionately kissing her. His remotely controlled left hand was around my shaft urging me towards her freshly manicured pussy. When Jason gets as horny as he was that night, then given any opportunity – and I do mean ANY opportunity

- he sends me into battle with complete abandonment.

"Just do it" he silently commands me. "Hurry up, hurry up" he adds as an afterthought. So, in I go, deep, deep, deep with no "begging-your-pardon, Ma'am". Julie-Ann just loves her sex a bit rough and because both Jason and I know this, we play to her carnal desires. In fact, it was my idea as we walked from the car park to send up a horny twitch or three to The Boss, giving him the idea that in this semi-lit area, with few pedestrians, that we could give her a special pre-dinner starter before proceeding on to the event.

I was in deep, right up to The Balls, and Jason was in no mood to take any longer than necessary for me to spill my contents. With her backside pressed firmly against the wall, this enabled Jason to thrust me in and out with sheer abandon. I was having a great time being used to my rugged masculine best, her muscles unable to squeeze me because of the lack of grip as I was thrust so quickly in and out of her warm tunnel. Fuck, it felt good being used and abused, exactly those same feelings she was expressing, when all of a sudden I came to an abrupt stop and was rudely exited backward into the night air.

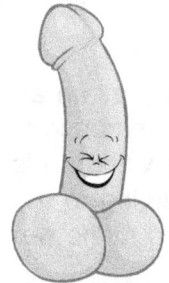

Ok! Ok! Looking back on it, I admit that I should have had more self-control, but in my defense, I was just at that point of no return. Shooting high into the air and all over the guard dog was quite simply not my fault! It was just a natural reaction to the sudden shock of me going eye-to-eye with the devil himself - all pointy ears, steely eyes, slobbering tongue and a mouth full of angry white fangs. It's just surprising that I didn't instantly recoil right back into Jason's pubes rather than continue vomiting my love juice all over said guard-dog Stanley.

Well, telling the truth, I did shrivel right back into Jason's body as quickly as I could after my projectile vomits into His Hairiness. The look on that dog as he recoiled away from me is a memory I'll keep forever.

If I do say so myself it was a grand sight as the creamy white thread thrust across the darkness, it's color and substance being captured by the beam of the flashlight.

"Aw fuck!" cried his master, the young security officer, as he too reeled back in fear of flying jizz. Really, it only hit his trouser leg, so I don't know what all the after-fuss was about. A wet sponge and I'd be gone without leaving a stain. But no, the scene as I peeped out of my now recoiled position, was like a disaster zone.

Julie-Anne had had the sense to pull up her knickers and lower the dress, but Jason was being held by another security officer, a woman, with his hands behind his back, his jocks and trousers still around his knees - and there's me dripping my bonus drops for all to see. With all the arm-waving and name calling you would have thought that some major robbery or treasonable offense had been caught in the act, rather than just a little bit of hanky-panky hot sex.

By now Stanley the dog was being wiped dry by an attendant and was still cowering a little over the surprise of it all. Security Officer Rob was like a child without his promised allowance money sitting there pointing to the stain on his trouser leg - continuously pointing to the wet cum stain area!

"This is a NEW uniform" he whined. "And my spare ones are at home."

"Just tell anyone who asks, that Stanley was a bit over affectionate and licked your leg" proffered Jason as a workable solution to the seemingly insurmountable horror scenario that Rob was reliving time after time in his head. That solution did NOT go down well.

"Shit, pull his trousers up will you" Rob responded as his keen eyesight rested directly on weeping me. "I don't want to look at that dipstick any longer. Just get him dressed and outta here."

As the jocks were pulled up it all went blank for me shortly after that. Fortunately, Jason was one of the important speakers at that night's event, so it goes without saying, that no charges were pressed. In fact, he, I and Julie-Anne were personally escorted by another security guard into the main auditorium as shattered Rob did not want to show his face or his still wet trouser leg to the waiting public.

Knowing that they could now get away with anything that night, The Boss, I and Julie-Anne slipped quietly away from the ceremony and we made love in that linen room we spoke about earlier.

That night, thanks to my copious outpourings, there was a second stain left at the hotel - this time in a place sure to surprise the room attendant the next morning!

******

Tara was an older woman, about a decade older than Jason. She'd got involved in the world of finance and was soon being head-hunted by several of the bigger corporation's head-quartered overseas. She loved the lifestyle that money and power gave her, and she loved to wield that authority with any and everyone around her. That was also carried through to her private life.

Jason had seen photos but didn't meet Tara until the wedding day.

The wedding was held in a stately mansion surrounded by beautiful gardens. It was an outdoor ceremony followed by the cocktail hour and then a gourmet meal in the exquisite ballroom. As well as the two bridesmaids there were two groomsmen, Jason being one of the latter.

Jason was very smartly dressed in a tuxedo, with a bowtie, black trousers and white shirt. I even got to be carried in brand new tightie-whities purchased especially for the occasion.

"Well, Young Jase, you never know your luck in a big city," he said to me as he slipped some condoms into his coat pocket. "Let you and I be prepared for a frustrated young housewife or a randy bridesmaid." And how prophetic that statement turned out to be.

With a quick clasp of me, adjusting me into a more comfortable sleeping mode within the jocks, he slipped the ring into the pocket with the condoms - and we were off downstairs to the waiting garden ceremony.

Sleeping in my pristine pure white pouch I could only hear the ceremony as it unraveled but it seemed that there was one very embarrassing moment. As Jason was fumbling for the ring in his pocket he accidentally dropped one of the unused condom packets onto the carpeted dais on which the wedding was being performed. That caused more than a titter of laughter as well as a "watch out girls" comment from Tom who was sitting in the third row. When that unscheduled moment subsided and the ring was finally firmly in place, the rest of the ceremony went smoothly.

As he told it later, when Jason reached down to retrieve the misplaced packet, he accidentally caught her eye - just for a second, but they did lock eyes. It was right there and then that both Tara and Jason knew that sex between them would be inevitable later that afternoon. Although no words were said between the pair, I got a very definite "yes, we have contact Houston" wake up message from The Boss, alerting me to the developing situation.

There were photo sessions and smiley greetings and laughter and happiness - all the elements that are indicative of a successful and glamorous wedding.

"You'll be next," said Andrew, thanking Jason for his part in being a groomsman. "Now that I've left the playing field, it's all yours. And I know that the right woman is out there waiting for you". And with that, he gave a double hand pat to his jacket pocket and a wink across to Jason. "Know what I mean bro?"

Both knew that Jason was a bit of a playboy and that any discussion about settling down "with a good woman" wasn't going to happen just yet.

I can attest to that!

After cocktail hour and the first course of the dinner, but before the speeches, the dancing began, along with more mingling and chatting and drinking. As it was traditional for the groomsmen to dance with the bridesmaids, I soon felt myself being pushed gently against an upper leg and what I predictively knew, it was female anatomy, most probably the subject of what I'd been tweeted to earlier in the afternoon. When I heard Tara's name I was immediately into "prepare and stand-by" mode. I tweeted The Balls in order to wake them up from their warm repose and to, in turn, fire-up The Sperm Factory. Knowing the speed that The Boss can move in order to achieve sexual conquest there wasn't a moment to spare.

And how right I was. Before the music segued into the second track I was being pumped into semi-erection and pressed even harder against her body. I suspect that she was impressed with my enlargement because very quickly the dance music started to fade away as I was walked upstairs. The click of the door lock behind me and her hand vigorously grasping my shaft confirmed the immediate attraction.

In my trade, this was going to be known as a quickie, pure lust, blow and go.

The sound of the zipper opening confirmed all of my thoughts. As his jocks were pulled from his body the light from the well-lit bedroom blinded me. Then WHO-AH! - straight into pitch black darkness as I was consumed by a totally hungry mouth. Up down, up down - if there was ever a case for over-enthusiastic molestation of a man's member, it was that afternoon. Tara was all action along my entire length. I have to admit that she was REALLY good at bringing me along, so much so that I had to let Jason know that if he wanted pussy action then he'd better get me out of this oral darkness and into her coochie - PRONTO!

Did I see as much as three-seconds of room light before I was plunged into coochie heaven? I doubt it. With dress lifted up and her legs apart, Jason swung me towards her wet waiting vertical smile, took a step forward and I was plunged in - DEEP! There were no regretful statements uttered, just pure animal lust at its best. She wanted me, and Jason was more than excited to give me to her. I was the sausage in the middle, giving pleasure through my mass of excited nerve endings to him and rubbing my head and length against her pleasure rock bringing her on towards orgasm. It was "all systems go" for the three of us.

Not one of us stopped our feverish activity for even a split second. But that meant I was being pushed and pulled and squeezed by the both of them without any regard for what was happening internally within me. Something had to give and you could be absolutely sure that it was going to be ME. I telegraphed my soaring point-of-no-return signal to Jason so that he'd be ready to give me that last deep, deep thrust or two. In the blink of an eye back came the message I'd been waiting for - and in I was sent for those final deep thrusts.

I released my pent-up juices deep into her warm caverns. Her muscular twitches around my head pushed me even deeper into spewing my contents, over and over again. Suddenly Jason's whole body was spasming into a rigor mortis-like statue position. He'd thrust me and his whole body forward with such force and abandonment, that he just collapsed over her like a spent athlete after a give-it-all track and field event. His whole body was heaving from the exertion he'd given and I was simply left to linger inside the cockpit until he'd gained his breath again.

With great effort, he pushed his body away from her and I slipped out in a state of semi-erection, gleaming in the room-light and still dripping a few of my love beads.

She lowered her dress and dropped to her knees. She

was still so turned-on that she needed – no, demanded - to have my last vestiges of tasty delights in her mouth. With deft tonguing movements, they were soon hers. She took my head into her mouth - but honestly, I was spent. The Balls and I had given our all and we had not a drop more to eject. Still, all this tonguing sent Jason shouting and squealing like a headless horseman, or more precisely, a groomsman with his dick caught in the church door....

"No. No. Fuck. Fuck. Fuck. No more. P-l-e-a-s-e..... Oh, fuck'n hell" he cried, seeking mercy and release from her controlling mouth exercise. Her mouth held on to my knob for a few more seconds before she mercifully released me, therefore giving Jason the release he also craved.

"Fuck, that was intense," he said to her with a wide smile, his breath still being caught.

"Meet you back here after the speeches" she replied, "I want more of that beast between your legs. Best shag I've had in weeks."

As Jason gently placed me back into his jocks for a well-earned rest, I was imagining the smile that was no doubt on his face. He simply adored being acknowledged that his dick was a fine specimen and as its owner, he knew precisely what to do with it to make women happy.

Ok, no direct acknowledgment of my part in all this, but hey - I know who controls the real strings during sex. Resting between bouts I smiled too, just knowing that my best friend (yes, I can call him MY best friend just as much as he can give that name to me) had a lot more enthusiastic sex for me to participate in, not only today but for seemingly endless years to come.

As I lay snuggled into his pouch I did a little internal squeeze and dribbled just one little pearl of happiness into his jocks right at the moment he was beginning his speech.

As a result, he might have fluffed his opening lines, especially the ad-lib about misplacing the ring and the consequent condom-packet-on-the-carpet moment, but the silent tweet back to me indicated that he did recognize that I was still in charge and that we were on a promise for later!

"Drip away old son – if you must - for this speech will be brief, as we have many more lustful pleasures ahead of us before this wedding day is over. Heaps more bareback skin-on-skin delights await us... just look around the room", he silently tweeted back.

"Well, no, Jason, I can't actually see around the room due to my tightie-whitie constricting circumstances" I wanted to tweet back, but because I do have a wild imagination when it comes to sexual pleasuring, then I knew that my rest period would be short-lived. And indeed, it was. Not only was there a Tara re-run, there were two others – one in a guest bathroom, the other in the darkness at the far end of the gardens.

Late that night (no, just after sunrise), the condoms were returned to the condom basket, unused. Both Jason and I flopped back on the bed exhausted. It had been the best (read: horniest) wedding that we'd ever attended.

PETER BENN

A medical salesman told me he had a foolproof way of making my dick a foot long.

I said, "Piss off, you aren't cutting nothin' off it!"

PETER BENN

CHAPTER SEVEN

THE CUM COOKBOOK

It had been a relatively quiet night of drinking at the sports bar when Andrew arrived carrying a plain brown paper bag with something in it shaped like a book.

And indeed, it was.

"CUM AND GET IT: 51 Delicious Recipes for Semen".

To say that the seven guys around the table went into meltdown upon seeing the book would be an understatement. They were transfixed by the very concept of its contents. Every shade of reaction from "fuck me" to "I don't believe it", and from "Yuck" to "We gotta try THAT" was expressed.

Who would have thought that the worldwide availability of the creamy juices we penises and our friendly accomplices The Balls produce could so divide such macho men? To me, its production and delivery is what I take part in every day. That's my main reason for living (apart from playing hose-host to the watering system of course). As professionals, my team and I produce, store and deliver the tastiest juice from the finest ingredients and it's always freshly made before I release it to my waiting public. Sure, a lot of it gets wasted in urinals, tissues, dirty sox or artificial latex vaginas but with Jason's enviable, though draconian production schedule, there's never a downtime, so it's always available 24/7. And I and the team pride ourselves on that.

I've rarely ever heard any complaints from the recipients of my natural whiter-then-white ejaculate. Most of the girls who taste it enjoy the sweetness (that's mostly caused by Jason's love of pineapple juice) so when Andrew exclaimed...

"I don't want to knowingly taste anyone else's juice" I was a bit put out. How would he know he wouldn't like it if he didn't at least try it?

"Eating some other guy's cum is just so gay" he continued. "Sorry guys, I just couldn't do it."

Jason added, "It says here, that jizz, as well as including a good dollop of our little swimmers, is filled with fructose sweetener just like in fruit, as well as citric acid, vitamin C, zinc and calcium for fighting tooth decay as well as other bits and pieces. Sounds tasty to me - and healthy!"

"Who wants a fresh load to mix with the beer" chimed in Jerry indicating that he was ready to whip out his dick-piston right there and then, and add to the froth of the glass.

"Awe, piss off, Jerry" Andrew replied.

"I can do that too if you want".

The night was now getting raucous and loud. Other tables were getting in on the conversation resulting in the most verbal abuse that I and my other appendages in attendance, have ever heard. This was cum-abuse of the worst kind. EVERYONE seemed to have a story about cum, its use, and abuse, its taste, its health benefits, its yuckiness, its skin beauty benefits, its cream-pie addiction, its amazing projectile abilities, its never-been-thought-of-before-food-supplement possibilities.

My fellow appendages - and I speak on behalf of them all - that night were trapped inside jocks and boxers unable to escape hearing such relentless mirth about our lifestyle and abilities. It was as if those humans, predominantly male, were the voices of an alien civilization crucifying the very workers and our amazing abilities to continually produce, stock and maintain at the ready, the cum that they rely on for their macho image and lovemaking reputations. We were all so annoyed that we were not being appreciated nor had we a way to voice our side of the story.

Eventually, the original table of seven decided that they needed to make a meal and drinks from the rich resources they carried within them. But perhaps experiment first before sneaking it into the meals with the girlfriends. Andrew bowed out, but the other six confirmed

"Next Saturday afternoon, at Jason's apartment. BYOC.

"What's BYOC?" asked Jerry.

"Bring Your Own Cum" Jason laughed back. "We'll need lots, so juice up every chance you get during the week and then freeze it in ice-cube trays. The book says that's a great way to store it. And we can make additional fresh on the day" he added.

"And who's going to be the one to milk me like a cow" added Tony. "You Jason?"

That caused roars of laughter as the taboo thought silently swept through the group mindset about other guys touching any other man's willy. Now that was TOO gay a thought for most of the group to cope with (at least in any public sense, but who knows what guy/guy action thoughts lurked under those laughing facades).

Saturday afternoon finally came around. Jason was intrigued by the whole potential of the afternoon. He and I had worked diligently during the week producing an ever-growing supply of juice for freezing. He'd read the book from cover to cover and was blown away by the variety of ideas and taste temptations. During that week, he'd lovingly wiped a finger-laden taste treat from me several times to weigh up the pros and cons of whether my juice was sweet enough, too sweet or just right. Now he would get the chance to try and compare other guy's taste sensations. And that excited him. Already the ice-cube tray was sitting on the bench defrosting in readiness. And the porn was playing on the television just in case stimulation for more fresh supplies were required later in the afternoon.

"Clothes off," said Jason to the first arrivals. "This is a clothes-free kitchen."

That was a bit of shock to the guys, but it felt right. They would cook better if it was like a natural sexy environment, was Jason's thought. It also meant that I got a full eye's view of the proceedings so that I could relate it all to you, so no objections from me.

The two ice-cube trays of melting cum lined up on the

kitchen bench perhaps looked more like a fourth-grade science experiment than a serious attempt at cum cuisine.

"We need to start with a drink," said Jason, knowing full well that any "ickiness" thoughts would be tested with their first sip, as would any revulsion from knowing that you'd be drinking someone else's juice.

He had already decided that first off, the cum had to be hidden within something else of a white creamy nature - and that was going to be a traditional Pina Colada.

A Pina Colada not only uses rum as the basis, it also includes a goodly dollop of coconut cream, so what better mixer to include man-juice in? It's also a great cocktail to loosen the inhibitions.

"Ok guys, while your own syrup supplies are defrosting I've prepared mine earlier in readiness for this first amazing cocktail. Here, hold this mug of coconut cream while I ease in a few defrosted cubes..."

The silence of that moment was deafening. It was like waiting for a disaster to unfold before their very eyes. It was as if not one of them could actually believe what they were taking part in. With a small but far from silent "plop", in they slid, one white-juice dollop at a time.

I could see the facial winces as each cube's contents slid into their milky grave. The guys were transfixed at the sheer audacity of what they were witnessing. Mesmerized by total disbelief.

"Ohhhhhhh - f-a-r-k...." spoken almost silently and very reverently, was quickly followed by....

"I. Just. Don't. Believe it," with every word being slowly and deliberately enunciated.

Everyone in attendance was by now totally wide-eyed and gob-smacked. If the world had ended at that moment they would be the most noticeable group waiting at the Pearly Gates - it was like wild deer caught in headlights.

"Give it a gentle stir" instructed Jason to Jerry.

The audible sigh of relief from the others who had not been chosen for the task was measurable.

Jerry slowly picked up the whisk, even more slowly lowered it into the cream and turned, looking for emotional support from his brother masturbators.

"Well, come on," said Jason, "start stirring."

It was only when he heard the sniggers of laughter that he realized what he had just said. That "come on" was enough to break the emotional ice and so the afternoon of experimentation moved into a more relaxed and adventurous one.

"Who's first?" asked Jason to the assembled classmembers, each now holding a tumbler full of creamy contents.

There were timid glances all round before the consensus of opinion was given - "All for one and one for all".

And with a rousing "Down the hatch" and a clinking of glasses, that's how the guys bonded even more firmly as macho "brothers forever". Few frat initiations had ever been this much fun, though of course, so many of those initiations did, in fact, involve a cum juice factor. The difference was that this time they WANTED to taste it rather than being FORCED to eat or drink it.

"Tastes good," said one. "You'd never know the secret ingredient was there," said another.

"Jason Juice tastes R-E-A-L nice" confirmed another. "It's definitely worth bottling and putting on sale!"

I was so pleased with that compliment. How wonderfully reassuring it was for me that my loads were being appreciated for the health-giving energy supplement that they are. Now, "bottling" my juice is something I hadn't considered. Perhaps that could be the basis of a new line of gourmet foods for the refrigerated section of the supermarket. And yes, I do like *"JASON JUICE"* as our trade name!

"Why don't we surprise the girls and get them all over here for a "special" meal tonight," said Jason. "We needn't tell them anything until after they've eaten."

"I can't," said Tony, "already got plans. But won't they be suspicious of your motives for suddenly deciding to cook for them?" he added.

"Absolutely – and that's why we have to say that someone's mother at this late hour, unexpectedly gave us all this left-over food to eat up."

'That's plausible" added Jerry "I'd believe that - one hundred and ten percent. Here, at eight o'clock then?"

"Can't wait 'til we tell 'em what was inside. It's gonna be awesome."

With a few phone calls, the dinner was confirmed with two of the current partners. Jason invited the lovely Amanda, and Jerry invited Mary-Anne.

"Might get a foursome out of it if we're lucky bro" added the naive and overly optimistic Jerry. "All that juice should do the trick for a late night thank you party. Wink. Wink. Maybe we can give each of them an extra juicy freshly-made, top-up mouthful just to finish the night..."

I could but cringe and shrink to my smallest capacity as I listened to all this macho discussion and vocal drivel. What land of relationship fantasy had they landed on – DimWit Island, Jerry and Jason's Land for the Perpetually Stupid or was it just another one of our regular visits to The Kingdom of High Hopes and Unreal Expectations. Did they have no idea of how traumatized the girls would be when they discovered the duplicity?

Obviously - and absolutely, NOT!

I felt it deep within my very molecular structure that tonight I would have very little to do until finally in the early morning, an exasperated and desperate hand would reach for me for a bit of rumpy-pumpy before falling asleep – alone - in his bed. That's the thing about being attached to the young, dumb and perpetually horny – the penis is always the first and/or the last line of his satisfaction scale. He's always in need of (1) a stiff, steel-like muscle-sword to conquer the vagaries of a tantalizing vagina or, (2) failing that, being the last line of masturbatory meatiness that can always be called upon to rise to the occasion to give solo satisfaction and guarantee sleep. One way or another we're ALWAYS in demand whatever the time of day.

And so, the afternoon continued as the newly inspired cooks decided on their menu and began its production:

Pre-Dinner drinks – Pina Colada - with cum mixed into the coconut cream

Nibbles – with cum in the mayonnaise, the cheese, and the trout dips

Main Meal - Meatloaf – where cum was added as an extra binding for the minced meat as well as into the accompanying gravy

Dessert - Lemon Chiffon Pie – where egg whites and cum juice were beaten together to form a foaming lemon mousse base

Irish Coffee – more cum beaten into the cream topping

I and the other afternoon penises were astonished at the enthusiastic efforts that were being put into this meal. As you can imagine, human food has little to no interest to me other than knowing when:

- on the menu, there are oysters (definitely need to then prepare for a busy night of exercise) or asparagus (well, what can I say other than life as a penis most definitely can have its downside!)

- blue tablets are being handed around and swallowed for late night erectile experimentation (you have no idea how exhausting it is to be erect for hours on end with little or no relief from the constant activity)

- or when the level of beer drinking is such that I

have little to do other than turn off the erectile muscles and lie back limply and receive a thorough flushing.

As they progressed in their preparations it became obvious that there was going to be a shortage of the one vital ingredient that was the whole rationale for the meal.

With a beer in hand, porn on the big screen television and six naked mates, what better way to continue enjoying the afternoon than a mutual masturbation jackoff session to collect more of the "secret ingredient".

As we six appendages were carefully directed to shoot our contents into the container in the middle of the circle jerk, I had nothing but the widest, happiest grin on my face. Where else would you find six happier naked chefs manufacturing, sourcing and collecting the finest and rarest ingredient for their next gourmet dining experience?

The evening went well - right up until the Irish Coffee. Of course, I could only hear all this, but the two girls were suitably impressed with "Jason's Mum's Food" even taking photos of it on their cell phones. The food was tasty, the wine flowed, lots of laughter – all the right vibes that would usually lead me to expect a busy night ahead.

"Jerry, come help me get the coffees ready," said Jason. And into the separate room that is the kitchen they went.

When they were alone, the conversation, driven as usual by too much alcohol, soon descended into self-congratulatory laughter and back-slapping.

"Do you reckon they suspected?" said Jerry.

"Absolutely no way bro. And what about them asking for

second servings of the pie" replied Jason as the two high-fived each other in agreement.

"Who knew that jizz could taste so good" added Jerry as he performed an exaggerated wank in front of his shorts.

The two girls were, of course, intrigued to hear all the laughter and exuberance emanating from the kitchen. They instinctively knew that their dates were planning something, whether with or without them.

It was Jason who looked up from Jerry's wanking exhibition to see Mary-Anne standing in the doorway looking aghast at what she had just heard and seen.

"What do you mean "jizz tastes so good"," she asked in a high-pitched quizzical voice.

"WHOAAA! How long have you been standing there..." said Jason, like a naughty schoolboy caught in the act of breaking rules?

"Are you planning to put something like your cum into those coffees you're making? Or even worse, have we already eaten something that has already had your cum included in it?"

"Trust me, it's not just MY cum" blurted out Jason. "The other guys gave as well!"

"WHAT. OTHER. GUYS! How many of you are involved in all this?"

By this time in the conversation, and I use that word loosely, Amanda had joined Mary-Anne in the grilling of their partners.

"Just a few of the guys from the bar. You know, the ones from the other night who were passing around the cum cookbook. We all shot a load and mixed it all up, so you weren't really eating anyone's juice in particular."

Jason continued, digging himself and Jerry into a deeper hole and from what I could hear, it wasn't going well for a potential foursome anytime soon. I rested in the knowledge that my predictions were all coming to pass.

'Don't you think that you should have warned us first. Telling us that it was all your Mum's food – what a friggin' lie".

"Yeah, I guess so. We should have been totally upfront" said a distraught and shamed Jerry.

"Damn oath, you should have been. If you wanted us to enjoy the experience as something downright special, we needed to understand all the effort you went to, especially for us. Don't you realize that NO-ONE has EVER presented us with such an extraordinary meal? We LOVE the taste of cum when you guys shoot it fresh into our mouth so why wouldn't we want to see what it tasted like when used as an ingredient in cooking?"

Did I just hear a seismic shift in the way the evening was now developing or have I totally lost my grip on reality?

"How would we have been able to enjoy such a gastronomic treat if we didn't know how much you cared for us. Guys are so timid about anything to do with cum, especially touching it and tasting it, whereas we girls just love it for all its skin softening and vitamin enriching qualities. Like Amanda said, no-one has ever cooked with it for me, so now I've got a great conversation starter for when I next see the girls for coffee. Also, can't wait to put the photos up online – and buy copies of the book as hints to future boyfriends."

"Show me how you're going to make the cream to top the coffee…"

Suddenly and totally to their surprise, there was now animated conversation including much laughter at the excess cum-cube storage in the freezer and describing how the fresh cum in the small bowl in the general part of the refrigerator had been collected.

From deep within that hole in the kitchen floor that Jason had dug so aggressively, both he and Jerry were now climbing out into the new world of Wonderland-Cum-Lately or was it Culinary Cumbinations. Whatever it was - the mixture of alcohol or the decadence and taboo of the subject matter - when combined with the lateness of the evening, began working its magic.

Much to everyone's surprise – and especially mine – I received a strong tweek from The Boss to indicate that the night was yet young. Standby for imminent action and prepare a hot load of man juice for at least one culinary gourmet expert for tasting – perhaps two!

Oh, how badly I under-estimated those young women. I'll hang my head in shame – again - but you'll have to wait until tomorrow for that. Tonight, I'm on duty and I know it will be a l-o-n-g high-octane night of multiple orgasms! I'll need to keep my head hard and high throughout for that.

Let everyone party and enjoy the sweet, freshly tossed, jizz-nectar directly milked from the two culinary whizz-kids. It was going to be a healthy night of juice-enhanced debauchery for the four of us.

PETER BENN

What's the difference between "ooohh" and "aaahh"?

About three inches!

PETER BENN

CHAPTER EIGHT

THE DREADED ZIPPER INCIDENT

The Dreaded Zipper - yep, caught like a rat in a trap. Well, you've never heard such a screaming and a-wailing, not to mention the blood, the hospital emergency visit, and the stitches. But then - oh my, then came the dinner conversations, the photos on the cell phone, the outpouring of sympathy from everyone - including his buddies, who recoiled in absolute horror that they were seeing something that could only be called nightmarish, something they knew was feasible but hopefully totally beyond any possibility of ever happening in their own lives.

Sure, some were impressed with my size, but mostly HE got the sympathy. The guys talked about "his" bravery (shouldn't that have been stupidity). The girls giggled and mentally compared me to their own lover's equipment. And then, and THEN, right there in the bar, he jumped up onto the table and whipped me out in all my bruised and battered glory for all to see (well, admire actually). The collective gasp was so loudly audible that it killed all other conversation.

And so began an intensive eye-height, eyeball-to-eyeball inspection of me by a myriad of strangers.

Why is it that when there is something on offer that's a curiosity, that people HAVE TO TOUCH IT in order to believe it? I've never had so much attention, and me being at my worst since that first week after the circumcision just after my birth. Not my best look, even though it's an amazing feeling being the center of attention – and so much better than getting no attention at all! Everywhere I looked there seemed to be a phone taking a selfie shot of me that I guess was almost instantly sent out to a waiting digital world as a warning to all other males that zippers can strike at the least expected moment and cause such carnage as I represented.

The men didn't really want to touch the horrendous crash-scene they witnessed before their very eyes, curious that they might have been as to how tender I was. It was the women, with their long fingernails and bachelorette stripper party curiosity that could not hold back. The Balls were fondled, my shaft was prodded, the bandage over the stitches was felt - there was a sense of close-up awe and wonderment the like of which that bar had never seen before.

"Does it hurt?" they silently wondered but then, not being able to control their intense curiosity, they asked aloud that very question.

"DOES IT HURT...." I silently screamed back at them. "DOES IT HURT?" I repeated. What the fuck do you think? I ask you - I'm black and blue, I'm bandaged, I'm stitched together - what the fuck do they think is going on here. I'm a shafted disaster, unable to perform my manly duties, unable to erect without considerable agony. Don't they realize that this IS worse than childbirth, worse than pulling wisdom teeth? It's so bad that my balls are filling up to overflowing through a lack of action and the worst thing that could happen is to have a spontaneous erection or worse still, have a wet dream. Just urinating has been enough to get Jason close to tears.

Fortunately, with all these women admiring Jason - and me – he exercised extreme mind control not to let anything about me grow beyond slack.

As he smiled and chatted and thanked everyone for their "tea and sympathy" I could just about hear him thinking of anything but sex - "my dirty sox need washing", "I must return the library book", "is it my turn to do drinks?"

Jason could read their expectant faces, so he decided that a diversionary tactic was called for.

And with "Drinks all round. My shout" I was no longer the center of attention. The fact is, he shouldn't have digressed in his thoughts.... for that moment of weakness in thanking everybody by buying drinks for the whole room, cost him nearly half his week's wages.

As the main body of the crowd moved hastily towards the open bar, I was gently returned to his loose-fitting boxers (jocks were just too snug for his pain threshhold). As the jeans began to be pulled up from the ankles, there was another hush from those still observing me. Would the Revenge of the Sharp-Toothed Zipper-Wolf strike again and this time would they all be first degree witnesses? Would I again fit neatly into the denim without causing my owner to shriek or whimper? Would he get an erection or at least crack a semi and then have to try to gently place me back into the jeans without so much as a muffled scream?

Those few moments of me being in the spotlight and of being a curiosity to the bar drinkers had peaked. All that remained of my minute of media fame and notoriety were the photos now digitally spinning across the globe in perpetuity. Go look – and no doubt you will find them. And when you view them let my cautionary tale be a warning to men everywhere – never – EVER – underestimate the painful consequences that a disrespected trouser zipper can cause to one's Johnson.

Very carefully Jason stepped down from his table pedestal making sure that I inflicted no further pain on either him or the Gonads Game Park in general. Healing was happening but not at the pace he desired. He didn't need any more delays in my recovery.

Looking back on the end of that night when the bar was closing it was just unfortunate that when Mandy pressed herself and her rather capacious handbag against Jason and myself when giving him a good-night kiss, that said handbag swung awkwardly, and with some force, crashed against bruised and tender me.

At the time, I was resting and half asleep.

Now... how shall I put this...?

It was like a sledge-hammer or battering ram being exercised against a soft cheesecake!!! And then, if you can imagine it, a surprise jack-in-the-box exploding out of a giant birthday cake to follow.

Yes, siree, the pain moved at lightning speed from tender don't-touch-me-under-any-circumstances straight through to Jason's pain center in his brain.

His scream stopped conversation throughout the bar. It

possibly also stopped passing traffic. And without a doubt, it certainly stopped any more sympathetic kissing.

As soon as we got home there was an immediate rummaging deep within the depths of the sporting closet. This continued until I heard the triumphant "I got it" response. And so, for the next week, I was totally protected by his hard-shelled athletic cup protector. Jason determined that no-one – and I repeat, NO-ONE, accidentally or on purpose, was going to get past this strengthened support receptacle in order to inflict me with any more pain. He'd had enough.

That night I slept soundly, with just the faintest dreams of feeling mass sympathy from empathetic men and fascinated women from across the internet when they discovered my photo on social media. And oh, yes, there was also that 3am shout from Jason when deep in slumber he accidentally rolled me under his body weight.

He didn't dare do that a second time!

PETER BENN

Q: Why do men have a hole in their penis?

A: (1) Because men are open-minded!

A: (2) So that their brains can get some oxygen now and then.

PETER BENN

CHAPTER NINE

THE ARCTIC BEARS

Like dicks the world over, we as a sub-species, all shrivel when exposed to the cold, especially to cold water and snow.

Therefore, a mid-winter dip in a cold ocean is not my, nor collectively, our scene. I need to share this story with you so that you'll appreciate how much I'm abused and not considered when decisions like this are made. For a guy who's always keen to show me off for my shape and size, sometimes Jason just doesn't think about my feelings or my sensitivities, or for that matter, the workload I undertake on his behalf.

And then to sit with his buddies over a beer or three or five as they make jokes about shriveled willies.... well, I ask you! Little wonder I hold myself back sometimes until I'm good and ready. After a morning dip like what I'm about to tell you, this is just another example of him thinking that *he's* in control of his sexuality!

I don't think so!!!!!

The Arctic Bears is just one of his buddy groups. They like to test their physical limits by doing what I would consider being seriously stupid extreme sports. (Just don't remind me of the naked bungee jump incident. The sheer terror of falling hundreds of feet through space still brings a shrivel to my inner manhood).

Of course, it's the beer that's doing the talking and it is at the bars where these wannabe alpha male macho guys do their planning.

"OK that's agreed - 6.30 Sunday morning, back beach, women welcome - and totally nude. And anyone who cracks a boner before 7.00 will be forcibly shunted back into the water. The weather guy on the TV says that it should be just a bit above freezing, so a great time to do it. Agreed?"

And the nine of them high-fived each other in agreement.

"Absolutely! Let's drink to that. And oh - bring beer."

Now as I see it, there are some fundamental elements in that statement that a sober man would consider as slightly fanciful - that these guys, all drunk and gung-ho, seem to have overlooked. What possesses them to think that any woman in her right mind would be standing on a lonely, windswept beach at 6.30 on a freezing cold morning wanting to watch a group of naked men bond in Arctic temperature waters? I suggest that it's perhaps not their ideal picture of romance and seduction.

When the 5.30am alarm goes off how many of the men will actually want to leap out of their warm bed knowing full well that they are about to torture their body with extreme cold. If they have one, will their sleeping companion offer encouragement knowing full well that she'd rather roll over and stay mercifully warm under the blankets than bond with ice-cold winds?

"Send me a photo", were her last muffled words that Jason and I heard before she slipped back into the bed warmth, pulling the covers over her head.

Naturally, every guy in the group *has* to go otherwise the shame of not turning up would be too shocking to live with. That's what buddies are for - doing things together, no matter how stupid or insane - and at whatever crazy hour is dictated. But really, all Jason wanted to do that morning was to stir me into action for another attempt at an overnight intercourse record. The apartment was really very warm and enticing, not to mention how enticing gorgeous Melanie was. She had been teasing me and swallowing me all night, both with her mouth and inside her velvet purse. That record was certainly within our grasp if only his mates weren't so insistent on everyone turning up at the beach.

I couldn't help but think about that ridiculous statement made in the sports bar earlier in the week - that is, "Anyone who cracks a boner...!"

Does he have *no* appreciation as to what cold water does to me and my performance ability? Doesn't he remember the "ice cube challenge" from college years or the sauna-and-then-running-into-the-snow-and-throwing-yourself-into-it episode up at the mountain cabin?

By hell, I do!!!!

The shock was enough to stunt my growth or at least hinder any immediate performance potential. Going from warm languid comfort to ice cold whammy is not for the faint-hearted. In one shocked movement, I quartered my size. Vrooom - right back into the warm, welcoming pubes I went. Lightning speed is what you might also have called it. It was like the recoil response when you touch something hot.

"FAAAAARK!!!!!!!!" was my master's cry as his hot naked body flung itself face-down deep into the snowdrift - with no regard for me whatsoever. And "FAAAAARK" all over again as one of his mates threw a bucket of snow over him - and consequently me.

Blinded by the snow and surrounded by its immediate cooling effect, all I could do was RETREAT!!!!!!

But then, with only my eye barely extending out from his pubes I was taken on a wild gallop with his mates as they whooped and hollered through the snow. It was Frost-Bite Central as far as I was concerned. I could see that his mate's penises had also taken the best shelter they could. Hoods were pulled over, others recessed themselves deep within their host body and I can assure you NONE - I repeat - NONE cracked a boner. Any potential boners were as deeply out of sight as they could get. There was barely a length of willy to be seen on any of them, just a series of slit-eyes looking out at men who should have had more respect for their sexual Best Friends. Tight sacs were the order of the day as they held the retreated testicles deep within the bodies. Nothing was exposed to the cold that didn't have to be. It was a scene where seven eunuchs seemed to be happily cavorting.

Fortunately, the extreme cold forces of Mother Nature were not too slow in getting the guys back inside the warmth of the cabin and under a hot shower. To my great relief, I was once again able to slide out and return to my natural extended position. Having The Balls tightly clasping against my inner shaft had been no picnic for me, so when the tight purse relaxed and they dropped back into place, what a relief!

Now at 5.55, it was the drive to the secluded beach. Darn, tootin' it was secluded. No-one in their right mind would be heading there at this time of the morning except this group of now quite sober young friends.

"Whose idea was this" questioned Gary as he got out of his warm car and caught the first frigid winds straight off of the ocean?

"Fucked if I know" replied Jason, pulling his coat tightly around his neck. Even through his jeans and the warm cotton jocks, I could feel the change of environment. I felt like screaming out "C'mon guys, show a bit of sense and stop this potential carnage on your dangly Best Friends. We're human too and frostbite or wind bite is not a good look. And then in a shouting voice they should definitely take notice of, I wanted to add.... "NO SEX FOR A FORTNIGHT GUYS. NOT EVEN A WANK. Think about it. NO SEX!!!!!!" I withdraw my services... DO YOU HEAR..."

My plaintiff cry must have got lost in the blustering wind, for alpha male Jerry was already herding the motley crew together for the group dash into the black freezing waves. The beach fire was already burning brightly; the beer was sitting on the sand (no refrigeration needed) and the towels were ready for a quick dry off after the fun. The what? THE FUN!

Jerry also had the idea of videoing it all, so he'd set up a camera higher up on the beach to capture the wide-angle action and then he'd use his cell to film the close-ups.

It was still dark, it was freezing cold, but the Arctic Bears or as known by some of us silent witnesses as the Stupid Nine had all rallied to the cause.

"Let's do it as a group - it'll be better that way," said Alpha Male.

And so, I and eight other very reluctant penises were thrust from the warmth of our traveling pouches and boxers and flung headlong into the spray-filled wind system. It was INSTANT withdrawal for most of us, though for some, our natural flaccid length simply had to hang down and take whatever the elements and our stupid masters wanted to fling at us.

It was a race to the water by the all-in, nine-man, nudist group. All this was accompanied by macho whooping and hollering that only a stray seagull got to appreciate. No-one was going to stop at the water's edge and put a toe in. Oh, NO! It was face-your-terror-full-on time and straight into the water. We splashed for a couple of steps through the shallows, and then by all that is valued, Jason dived head first into an incoming wave. If that stray seagull was still within earshot he would have heard me scream like I was again being circumcised without anesthetic.

"FFFFFFFFFAAAAAAAAAARRRRRRRKKKKKKKKK!!!

And I wasn't the only one. Eight other appendages screamed out much the same sentiment at exactly the same time. If you could have harnessed those shrill cries you would have been able to shatter glass.

TINDERfella

And immediately following that scream for mercy, you could almost imagine that you heard one incredible VRRROOMPH! as nine frozen dick shafts sought instant withdrawal back into fleshier, warmer body parts. If a huge ZIPPPPPP!!!!! is what you thought you also heard, then that was the ball bags shrinking back into VERY tight purses in order to protect their valuable bouncing cargo.

There was more whooping and hollering and abusive language that would have made that seagull blush to bright pink. The guys knew that they had to keep moving in order to retain any sense of body warmth as there was much group prestige to be had by being among the very last to leave the water. The honorary Annual Arctic Bear Chieftain title would be bestowed on the last to emerge from the frigid waves, with or without a boner. This award within the group also meant not having to pay for his beer on the first day of every month for the whole year. The boys considered this award to be highly prized and not to be lost to another member without a fight.

"GIVE IN JASON" I screamed. "Let's go and get warm."

But owners being somewhat dim-witted as they often are, had to slug it out in the near pitch black and the cold until there were only two remaining in the water - Jason and the current title holder, Jerry. Who would hold the senseless, but much sought after crown for another year?

As I looked up the beach from my nestled hiding spot deep within as much of Jason's body as I could squeeze into, all I could see were seven other young men toweling themselves dry as they stood beside the blazing fire, their actions beckoning us to also get out of this freezing

169

hell-hole and go and feel the warmth. As predicted by moi, none of them had a boner nor I suspect any likelihood of growing one any time while on the beach. My compatriots were all shrunken and hiding as best they could with their ball bag companions as tight as a purse can get. As they warmed up from the heat of the fire, they'd soon return to normal, but right now that was a thought that I was unable to comprehend. Another two minutes or even one more minute of that cold and I would be a dead prick, a useless asset to womankind. I tried to send that message up to The Boss. His whole body was shaking, the hairs were standing on end, the toes were frozen, the legs had little feeling left in them, the nipples were as extended and ripe for plucking as I'd ever seen them.

Then, without warning, Jerry caved into the cold and began a run out of the water and up onto the beach. In fact, he limped, for his legs had little feeling left in them and he stumbled a couple of times. The admiring audience left the fire and brought warm towels and a blanket to him.

The Boss and I had won the coveted trophy through sheer perseverance and will-power. He waved his arms up in triumph, the audience applauded and we began our trek back to the light and the warmth of the fire.

"What a legend," I supportively silently screamed, "that's my man, The Boss!" (Yes, I too can be a fickle dick and change my opinions on the turn of a screw).

While he was delighted at his macho achievement, I could only wonder to myself - "what next?" And then I remembered - Oh, yes, defending the title this time next year...! I drooped a little at the very thought.

How none of we nine penises didn't get chilblains, frostbite or PSS (Permanent Shrinkage Syndrome) I'll forever be grateful. The fire slowly warmed me as it did my brothers, and soon we all returned to our natural dimensions. That was fortunate, as the beer soon started to move through the respective kidneys and we were all called upon to stream forth. Jason and I didn't win either Furthest Whizz or Highest Draining the Vein, but we did give both a good attempt.

At 7.13 on a freezing winter's morning, I can't be expected to be at my best, especially when I know that there is a warm sex muffin waiting to play with me and Jason back at the apartment.

"Come on Jason, I telegraphed, "let's get dressed and get outta here. Civilization and warm sleeping pussy await."

PETER BENN

A father was advising his son to "Stop masturbating so much because if you do it too long you'll go blind."

The son replied, "Dad, I'm over here".

PETER BENN

CHAPTER TEN

THE NIGHT OF THE NIPPLE RING

I thank Jason for being a bit squeamish when it comes to blood and pain and the whole damn thing. Sure, the nipple ring incident was the turning point that said "no more body jewelry" but before that, it looked almost certain that Prince Albert and I were going to be a match made in heaven in the not too distant future. So, what was it that kept Prince Albert from inflicting me with his dazzling chrome-ringed circular beauty?

We were on vacation with his buddies when the fine art of body jewelry started to be talked about in a more serious way by Jason. A couple of the other guys had had their nipple rings for some time and they constantly talked about the intense feelings the rings and their movement gave them. There was initially some pain and inconvenience, but the pain was now a long forgotten after-thought. It was all about looking good, particularly as the rings emphasized not only the nipples but also the muscled pecs, and this, in turn, attracted admiration from women. The guys also didn't mind the attention and the stimulation that a voracious tongue could achieve on this sensitive area. And we all know how connected many nipples are to their Best Friend dangling below. I mean - a DIRECT line of stimulation that can iron-out a drooping dangle in quick smart time - and keep it from any thoughts of returning to a dangle until well after the business end of the hook-up is completed.

"We'll go now! The Pink Poodle Tattoo and Piercing Studio is open 24/7" said the alpha buddy. "It's better when you're drunk as you won't feel a thing."

The name alone should have rung warning bells, even in their advanced inebriated state. We were on vacation in this tropical backpacker backwater where everyone except the shop assistants was totally drunk day and night. Every young traveler existed in a state of euphoria and blind ignorance of reality, not to mention the additional support of a party drug or two or three that helped that situation perpetuate itself.

The gaudy neon sign that flickered two pairs of alternating poodle legs as if simulating their running was warm and welcoming at that early morning hour. The other group members who hadn't already pulled a bed partner for the night came to give their moral support. None of them took any notice of the cleanliness of the establishment or bothered to ask about the piercing experience of the young women who worked there.

"My friend here wants a ... what-do-ya-call-it ... nipplely ring thingy. Which nipple bro?" was the opening line from the quite drunk Eddie.

"Left one" Jason replied.

"Sure you don't want both done bro? It's about the same price."

"Nope! If it's going to fuckin' hurt as much as I think it will, I'll stay with one."

Hearing all this as I free-balled in his shorts, amazed me that the locals could actually understand drunken backpacker broken-English.

"If sir could just take off his top and lie back on the chair, I'll get things ready," said the therapist in broken English.

"Look calm bro. You're on camera so your future kids will be able to see how the old man took it like a trooper."

There were now seven interested onlookers all enjoying Jason's nervousness. Some knew from personal experience what he was about to endure, others thankful that it wasn't them in the chair. And of course, those from the buddy group had nearly all seen the infamous waxing video so they were again expecting a stellar performance of note from Jason.

I could feel the fear Jason had in him at that moment. She swabbed the nipple with something cold, probably pure alcohol, and then gave him two quick needle pricks to deaden the coming intrusion.

The forceps took hold of the nipple, stretched it out tight from his body, and then in went the needle. From what I saw on the endless video replays, Jason refused to look at what was happening and simply moaned out through gritted teeth a low rumble.

"GGGGRRmmmmmmm Oooooo - fuckin' hell", or some

such-like deep throat sound to that effect.

"No worries bro. She'll get it right next time." And the relieved group laughed.

The ring end connected to the needle, it was pulled through, end screwed on, a quick wipe with a cloth and he was done.

"Wow, that wasn't so bad," said a now somewhat more-sober Jason as he admired it in a mirror.

"Lady, I think he's changed his mind and he WILL get the second one done".

"No fuckin way man" and more laughter from all concerned.

"Let's get outta here."

"Just one-minute guys. I have to tell Mr. Jason here that no swimming in the pool or the ocean for two weeks - and don't use soap when you shower. The piercing will be tender for the next couple of days so be careful. Don't knock it on anything and don't let anyone suck on your nipple...."

"Awe man, you're grounded," responded Andrew.

"Thanks for nothin' bro. Do you really think that this little mosquito bite is going to stop me from scoring? No way man!" said Jason, pulling out all his overt masculinity from wherever it had been hiding during the last twenty minutes.

"Same bullshit advice after the waxing, and look how I kept scoring."

This was classic Jason – macho on the outside, while full-well knowing his nipple was as painful as hell and he was definitely going to respect it through the healing period. Still, with a bit of careful management, a sore pec wasn't likely to stop his winning way with the girls.

"You guys can go but I'm getting my PA," said Louis.

Suddenly the tone of the early morning changed from fun to deadly serious. Anyone it seems can get a nipple piercing and cope with the quick bite of pain but to get a Prince Albert, well, that is top of the heap for serious bro activity. You're a genuine alpha male to sport one of those little beauties. You're made of tough stuff and you know how to express your masculinity to not only your buddies but impress the women. Not being party to anything other than Jason having a nipple ring I can't speak for other penises and their owners, but that PA macho image seems to get serious street-cred.

"No man. You can't. There's still a week of willy-waving and scoring before we head home, and with your dick out of action who's going to want you? Let's do it as a group the first week we're home..."

"Ok. Absolutely. One hundred percent locked in."

And with a group high-five, we all dispersed back to the hotel to sleep it off.

Well, that was easier said than done. Jason and I normally sleep in the nude or at max have a tee on top. The walk back to the hotel along the beach was barechested as no way was any material going to touch that nipple. Even the warm night breeze passing over the top of it was enough to have that little baby standing erect and proud.

"Ahhh, Mr. Jason, you have a new piercing I see," said the night attendant. "Very sore me think" he added, teasingly raising his finger to touch it.

"Fuck off," said a very wary Jason as all the others broke into laughter at Jason's vulnerability.

In our room and now fully naked, Jason began the admiration routine. He looked in the mirror, he admired, he cleaned his teeth, he admired some more - and smiled the smile of a winner who had just achieved success for a long-cherished goal.

"But hey, what about me down here" I was tempted to signal. But for tonight at least, it seemed like I had been usurped by a bit of shiny bling.

I'm a patient penis, and I know my master very well. As you rightly guessed, it wasn't long before the tables were turned and I was being manhandled in order to give him some masturbatory relief, and therefore divert his attention from the pain before trying to capture some elusive sleep.

He was on his back, as any other position was impossible to contemplate. Pillows were plumped either side of him so as for him not to roll around during sleep and that meant that I was on display up front and center the whole time. He desperately wanted relief by way of a wank but even the hand reaching down for me stretched his upper torso and he winced in pain.

The messages he sent down to me ranged from the excruciatingly painful "Fuck. Fuck. Fuck." right through "Jeepers, I need to cum, I really, really do" and on into "I can't. I can't. I can't! It hurts too much."

But I did cum.

"Oh fuck, oh fuck, WHAT THE ...." he cried out in sheer horror as my creamy abundance shot high up his torso and scored a bullseye hit on his inadvertent nipple target.

Now, let me state categorically that it wasn't MY fault! HE was the one who was directing me. HE knows how powerful a cum shot I can produce. And HE shouldn't have been lying there so smugly thinking and admiring his new bling instead of paying attention to his long-serving associate between his legs. Aim me into a pillow, towards the wall, a towel, over his other shoulder - HE HAD A CHOICE!

If a huge hairy tarantula spider had appeared in the bed at that very moment of my shooting, Jason wouldn't have jumped higher or faster than he did when the first drop of jizz hit home.

"F-A-R-K!!!!!!!!!!!!!" he screamed, automatically leaping to his feet thus sending me spraying the residue to all four corners of the room.

And if that floor had been red-hot coals, he couldn't have leaped around more than he did.

I felt like I was in free-fall, being swung like a pendulum in every direction as every touch of his feet on the imagined hot coals sent him wildly off in another direction. It was a tribal war-dance that would have scared any enemy into immediate retreat or submission.

Suddenly the door flew open and in raced two of the

other guys. Having heard the screams through the thin walls they hurried to help their mate.

"What's up bro?" they shouted as they saw him leaping from foot to foot in a dance located somewhere between ecstasy and torture. No doubt they also saw me in semi-erection with a spider web strand of juice dangling from me.

"YOU-SHOT-A-WAD-ON-TO-YOUR-PIERCING!!!!!" Andrew shouted in total disbelief. "What the fuck were you thinking?"

"AAAAAAARRRRHHHHHHH" Jason responded in pain as Andrew grabbed hold of his shoulders in order to calm him but inadvertently stretching his torso at the same time.

"I couldn't sleep could I, and I needed to wank off to get relief. Oh, Gawd...." and with that, we headed for the bathroom. With all that tribal dancing, the latent alcohol of last night's drinking had been mixed one too many times in Jason's stomach. And so, we hugged the toilet bowl for the next ten minutes.

After the vomiting session, the guys sat Jason down, carefully - and VERY gently – washed the area around the nipple. My juice being so sterile wasn't going to cause any bacterial issues, but they cleaned it away anyway. It was more the shock rather than the possibility of infection that was being treated.

In due course, the guys got The Boss and me back into bed, carefully re-distributing the pillows to provide a confining coffin-like experience for him. There would be no rolling over during sleep and thus no more anguished screams to wake them before midday.

After such a rigorous, though unexpected, aerobic workout and an early morning like no other, I simply lay atop of my master and slept. With the coming of the daily noon brunch ritual I knew I'd soon become the focus of Jason's attention once again.

After all, what's a horny vacation without an overworked, oversexed Johnson in your shorts?

PETER BENN

*A patient asked his doctor for help for his
premature ejaculation issue.*

*A: "Only date women with a
short attention span" he replied.*

PETER BENN

CHAPTER ELEVEN

THE MISTRESS

Blind dates NEVER go the way that the parties expect.

There's always that awkward moment over dinner where...

HE silently sums up his situation - my place, her place, will she, won't she. Should I just pay the bill on the way to the bathroom and simply not come back. Who cares - just get me out of here as quick as I can. Why does she eat so slow, let's just leave and start the kissing and the fucking... Gawd, her breasts are so plump and inviting! Is she shaved, trimmed, au naturel?

SHE thinks - my place, his place, quick sex in the women's bathroom out back, why bother with this loser, how big is his wiener, how small, is he adventurous, or a potential dud root. Might as well enjoy the food then say goodnight and piss him off for some other poor woman to date. What stunning pecs, and my, my, those rock-hard arm muscles - what else is rock hard - and deliciously B-I-G?

And then there are sometimes more extreme thoughts from HER that could curl a man's toes. But best he doesn't know about those possibilities in advance – as this story will prove.

Roxy was one such blind date that will never be forgotten by either Jason or myself. As a self-crowned alpha male, The Boss upstairs likes to think he's in charge of our sexual encounters. He knows and appreciates that I'll perform for him under almost any circumstance, and as often as he calls the shots. With that aspect guaranteed, the way he sees it, all he has to do is find, romance and seduce his woman, gently guide her to the bed and they will share his love-making in whatever way he wants the encounter to go. Yep, he's the full chauvinist.

Well, he was, until Roxy showed him otherwise.

He'd met her online:

27yo slim experienced woman seeks similarly aged male for adventurous sexual times.

After a few messages and exchanges of cell numbers, the first date was organized. At HER place! She lived alone, had a professional career at the senior executive level, boasted a fine figure and seemed to have a natural authority about her that was both unusual and intriguing. Jason was hooked from the time of the first message.

"I know what I want and know how to get it. If you enjoy hot sex, then we'll get along famously. What turns you on?" she asked.

This role reversal added to the intrigue, and when she added "I'll cook" then it was a foregone conclusion that the following Saturday night was going to be anything other than ordinary, and I'd certainly be put to work at the earliest possible moment.

It was a five-star apartment building housing executive-type singles and older well-to-do couples. Jason was very impressed by the spacious foyer, the attentive staff and what seemed like a fair share of the entire world supply of marble tiling. Very luxurious!

Roxy opened the door and in we went to her spacious apartment. "This girl is obviously doing very well for herself", Jason thought, now also congratulating himself over the expensive bottle of wine he'd purchased specially for the occasion.

Her mode of dress should have given Jason a clue about how the evening was going to go. Sculptured leather leotard with shiny stud highlights, black textured stockings, an expensive watch with a huge supporting red leather wrist-band, bright red stiletto shoes with lipstick to match, hair in a bun and a metal necklace with just a single bronze key dangling from it. Everything was co-ordinated to emphasize her height and authority. From Jason's first sight of her, I was being given encouraging signals to prepare myself and The Balls for a lustful evening.

"Champers to begin with?" she asked.

"Whatever's going", he responded, thinking that a beer would have been more to his liking.

"Can you be a darling and open it for me?" she asked, giving him an encouraging kiss on the cheek and handing him the bottle.

And so, the drinking and the conversation began. The

lights were low, the candles flickered, the aromas were exotic. This was one classy lady, Jason surmised. And one with a sense of unique fashion style he'd not encountered before in his twenty-seven years.

Jason's wine was opened and poured, the meal was eaten, with conversation ranging from politics to vacation sex, from leather fashion to celebrity gossip, openly and in all instances, enthusiastically discussed. By the end of the meal, the heady mix of wine and champagne had loosened Jason's sense of reality and he was somewhat inebriated when Roxy excused herself from his arms and their passionate kissing.

"I just want to slip into something more comfortable," she added.

It was a classic line but not one that Jason had heard many times before.

"Take those clothes off and meet me in the bedroom, first room on the left".

As directed, he quickly slipped out of his clothes and began looking around for the missing Roxy. My first glimpse of the room showed me the luxury. Quality satin sheets, subdued lighting, a huge king size bed. Jason and I weren't used to such opulent surroundings. In eager readiness I was proudly on display in a semi-state of erection for I was keen to impress our hostess.

"Are you lying face down on the bed?' came the voice from another adjoining room.

We weren't, but quickly Jason got into that position, tucking me underneath, face down into the satin, his head into a pillow, his feet slightly dangling over the end of the bed.

"Ready," he replied.

"I'm coming. No peeping"

It was the unexpected "click" of the handcuffs joining the two ankles together that startled him.

"What the ...." Jason responded, half turning to see Roxy wearing a body-hugging studded leather bondage corset and carrying another set of the cuffs.

"Just a little fun darling. You said that you were sexually adventurous, so I'm here to help you live out your fantasies. Now, arms behind your back..." she added with a voice of authority.

"No. No.... "

"Oh, p-l-e-a-s-e darling, you'll have such fun, I promise you," she purred. "Now, give me a safe word, and when you say it I'll stop doing whatever I'm doing and release you. I won't harm you.... I promise."

"I'm not sure about this. This is all new to me...." stammered out Jason. But seeing her lower lip pouting as if hearing that she couldn't be trusted, he added "Ok, ok ... use .... uh... beer as that word."

"Beer it is" she confirmed, the pout now gone and the sternness returning. And with that Jason put his arms behind his back and his wrists were cuffed.

Even though I could hear and feel his racing heartbeat pounding through his body there was also very unexpected thrill messages being transmitted right into my central blood vessels. I was once more on the rise. The brain might be hesitant about this unexpected development in losing control, but the eroticism was palpable.

The Boss rolled onto his side, therefore, exposing me to the same view that he had...

Her hair was now swept up into a ponytail. The earrings and choker were links of a large silver chain. The lips - bright shiny polished red. The body-hugging black corset showed her body curves off to perfection. The ultra-brief black lace bikini bottom held up the matching black fishnet stockings which were in turn partially covered by high black patent leather boots with bright red toes and massively high stiletto heels to match the lipstick. The boots were a weapon in themselves as was the leather riding crop she was now holding in her hand.

Roxy was the first real dominatrix that either of us had encountered, and speaking for my now erect self, I was VERY impressed and made no effort to hide my adulation. She oozed confidence and an extraordinary sense of power and dominance, even menace. She had physical control of the situation, now she needed the all-important mental control.

"You will at all times refer to me as Mistress. You will not speak to me nor will you refuse my orders. I have here in my hand my whip, and believe me, if you fail to adhere to my demands or you speak out of turn or disrespect me, it will be used upon your body. Now - who told you to roll onto your side?"

"No-one. I just wanted to see you."

From my exposed position above the satin, I saw the

instant flick of the wrist as she responded her power-wielding riding crop onto his bare skin.

THWACK went the crop unexpectedly across Jason's right buttock.

"I AM MISTRESS! You will ALWAYS answer me by that name. Yes, Mistress. No, Mistress. Do you understand?"

A second THWACK hit the other buttock.

"Yes, Mistress. I'm sorry, I'm sorry. It won't happen again" he responded like a naughty schoolboy endeavoring to avoid additional punishment - and he rolled back onto his stomach squashing me once more into the satin. The shock of the riding crop hitting the bare skin temporarily had me diving back inside for cover. Pain has never been my friend and the shock had Jason sending me "Withdraw. Withdraw immediately" messages to which I didn't hesitate in instantly responding to.

"Now for the blindfold," she added.

Deftly she placed the silk tie across his eyes and tied it tightly behind his head.

Jason and I were now at her mercy. Neither of us could see anything, though our hearing was more acute than normal. We had no idea what our fate was to be. Would she want to have sex with a blindfolded, bound-up naked man with a shy willy averse to any form of pain? Of course, in hindsight, we should have known that it wasn't about HER having sex, rather it was about giving highly eroticized sexual pleasure to Jason.

But we certainly didn't know that from her first instructions.

"I'm removing your ankle shackles so that you can service me more freely. You are here to do my bidding and if it is not done to my complete satisfaction my jockey's friend will once again taste your bare skin. Now - on to your feet and facing me."

"Yes, Mistress."

I was once more able to see the room and Mistress Roxy. I was able to see her run her riding crop its full length along under Jason's nose.

"That's the smell of danger" she threatened. "Now, legs apart."

And with another deft flick of the wrist the end of the crop was under The Balls. Having parted them like a theater curtain she was now trying to lift them up, all the while putting pressure on the confluence of where they finished and I began. With a wicked wiggle of her leather wand, she made sure that they were awake to their job. They jolted a painful acknowledgment of her mastery over them.

Then she moved it to the perineum, that epicenter of manly delight between The Balls and Jason's rosebud. The handle-end of the crop stopped dead on target - and she began to intensely massage his P-Spot.

"MMMMmmmm..." he purred.

"WHAT DID YOU SAY" she commanded. "Did I hear you speaking without being spoken to?"

With a quick fluid movement, the riding crop struck a

blow to the leg.

And I could see all this happening right before my eyes! That menacing elongated leather baton with its thick, blunt, handle-end and its leather flap at the other came right at me. In my semi-rigid state, the leather flap slapped more than gently against my shaft. FUCK!!! - I was stung and went into immediate propeller mode. My shaft flapped around in all directions like a headless chicken trying to escape the wretched and immediate pain that had been inflicted.

"Geez" I messaged Jason, "don't for fuck-sake talk to her. I'm your fragile friend down here, and I'm the one taking this pointless beating. JUST SHUT UP, will you!!!!!!"

Amidst my blurry vision, I was confused. Should I harden up or grow soft? And what of this internal heat - well, really, the pain - generated within me from the slap?

Eventually, I managed to decipher the tangle of messages he was sending me. He wanted an erection - NOW!!!!

"What the ...." I responded. I was still stinging and here's The Boss wanting me immediately back in action doing his bidding. I was now really very confused - and painfully sore - yet so alive to the erotic environment, more so than I had been in a very long time.

I was still sorting myself out as to whether to open the blood trapdoors or to shrink back inside of Jason and temporarily withdraw from the battle when WHAMMO, a whole regiment of Erection Messages hit me like a thunderbolt from above.

She'd tweaked his nipples!!!!!!!!

Fuck, now there was no holding back. The decision had been made from Headquarters and we were in full erection mode. Wheeeee!!! I do so love life when my man and I are partners in unstoppable pleasure.

As you well know, touch Jason's nipples and I'm all yours - FOREVER! Trace a triangle between his nipples and down to the beginnings of my shaft, and you have the perfect erector mechanism. My mind loses any sense of good behavior and my internal brain lapses into a jellied muddle. I go into erection auto-pilot. There's not a chance-in-hell that while those nipples are being attended to that I'll do anything other than be the stiffy of your dreams and the pre-cum rivulet of delicious taste.

"On your knees, stiffy," she demanded. (Had she heard me telling you this?) "I do so like a man who has your qualities. Now let me see what you can do with your tongue..."

"Yes, Mistress" he stammered in reply, silently wishing that she should be more interested in getting him off rather than prolonging his now urgent desire to lose his load. I picked up on that silent message but could do nothing about it for the time being.

And with that, I watched her release her bikini bottom and bring her shaved nether-regions to his face.

"Smell me, boy. Sniff my snatch .... imagine what you could do to it if I was naked on the bed and you were unshackled.... come on boy, sniff me - and tongue me ...."

Sometimes a view looking upwards from where I'm situated can bring me additional untold pleasures - and sometimes a view of nostril hair that definitely needs a trim. That said, The Boss was like a puppy in search of a tasty bone or a tracker dog in search of illicit drugs. Indeed, the latter was most appropriate particularly as his tongue began to diligently undertake a complete internal body search. Oh, my jumpin' joy, he was totally getting into this. From a slow munch to a deep tongue bath he just went for it!

"DEEPER BOY" moaned Mistress. "use that tongue of yours, plow me with it, deeper...deeper..."

I could barely hold myself together through all this feverish activity that was happening up above me in her perfumed garden. The messages from The Boss were becoming ever stronger, ever more demanding, yet there was nothing to indicate a release forthcoming for me in the immediate future. As I peered up I marveled at the intensity of pleasure that a shackled man can inflict on a woman when he has the right encouragement.

Mistress's moans were getting stronger as he had obviously begun working on her clit. She now held Jason's head in her hands holding him tightly to her pussy, occasionally pulling on some of his hair in reaction to his excitable tonguing. Her legs were stiff and braced tight against his kneeling torso. The air above me was punctured with droplets and strands of saliva and self-lubrication falling to the carpet - and on to me.

After an additional short time of tongue-lashing and with one enormous moan, Mistress arched backward and screamed "Yes. Yes. Y-E-S-SSSSSSS!!!!", her mind soaring somewhere between Jason's tongue and the ceiling.

As reality began to return to the room she indicated that he and I should stand and then roll back onto the bed, his hands remaining cuffed behind him, and myself, now the center of her attention, pointing heavenwards in all my super pumped up glory.

She reached for a small bottle of spray. Before you could say "cumming, ready or not" I was a sprayed gooey mess. I began to grow cold, then to lose my sense of purpose, and my sense of feeling. It was as if I was becoming numb. As indeed I was. I'd been assaulted with "delay spray" in order to keep me in check and obviously not to shoot before she said it was ok to do so. Mistress was definitely still in total command of the situation and I was the unfortunate butt of her whims. Didn't she appreciate the delicate but enthusiastic pleasure-giver that I was, that I had a job to do whenever The Boss told me it was time to evacuate myself and give him - and her - good feelings?

Obviously NOT! For to douse me in a slimy substance that was more at home in a medical facility than a sexual playroom, and leave me with no self-control, was totally unfair and beyond anything I had ever had happen to me. I had a function to perform, one that I'd been able to regulate on my own and with The Boss's help for well over a decade, multiple times a day if necessary, and in the most diverse of amazing sexual locations. I was an experienced performer, a skilled professional, an elite athlete - and here I was a numb, jizz-filled, anesthetized lump of wiener sausage-meat ready to do my part in the evening's proceedings but now denied active participation and self-control.

Of course, I shouldn't have reacted so vehemently, but how was I to know that Mistress was going to give Jason the deepest, most meaningful orgasm that he had had up to that age. Without me appreciating it, she now also had ME totally under her control. Both Jason and I could only wait to see what she had in mind for us both.

This whole event was all about her control, her power over the male, her decisions about what would and wouldn't happen. For all that, Mistress had no intention of totally missing out on the pleasures that I could provide.

As we lay face-up on the bed, she stood above us like a towering medieval executioner, her leather-wear promising actions of no mercy, her trusty crop in her hands and her very wet pussy glistening in the subdued light - but not for long. She was on her way down toward me, toward getting herself into that ever-reliable squat position. I could see her wetness was descending and directly targeting me. Anesthetized I might have been, but I was going to be taken for a ride - bareback, skin-to-skin. With his arms cuffed behind his back, there was nothing Jason could do but to lie back and enjoy, his eyes taking in every sensual moment of being used and abused. I could see that he ached to be freed and then to reach out and touch those voluptuous breasts and kiss the warmth of those enticing bright red lips.

As I stood sentinel erect, ready for whatever fate was descending my way, it only took a single fluid movement and I was plunged into darkness. I knew it was warm and wet, yet I couldn't feel it. I was deep inside her, then back towards the entrance, then deep again - and I wasn't doing a thing other than maintaining the blood flow inside of me. Mistress Roxy was doing all the work. Even in my dulled mindset, Jason's messages kept getting through....

"Keep it up, young buddy. I can feel you working her,

filling her. Damn, I don't think you've ever been so hard, or so long or so thick. Oh, fudge, I'm going to have to blow real soon. But no, no, I don't want to as yet. Hold on, hold on as long as you can..."

The torrent of appreciation from Master Jason for my valiant efforts was not going unrewarded, it was just a pity that I was "high" on this mysterious spray drug and couldn't really appreciate the pleasurable abuse that her riding me was providing him. Still, I maintained the sense to simply keep the status quo, remain as stiff as I could and just let it all happen to me.

Suddenly, I saw room light again, and in the blink of an eye, I saw the crop briskly slap The Boy's nipples. FUCK!!! - even without most of my senses, I felt that message. I very nearly lost it.

She rose to her full height, lowered the crop toward me and gave a THWACK upon me like I've never encountered before. Obviously, it wasn't as painful as it could have been had I been in my normal state, but JEEEEEEZZZZZ!!!!!!! It fuckin' tossed me W-A-YYYYYYY over the top. I didn't even have to wait for the muscle reaction from Jason before I spewed.

He screamed a huge, deep baritone F-A-RRR-KKKKKK and I shot like an out-of-control circus cannon - nothing was spared. Way past his ear and onto the satin pillow, more for his face, all over his pec. It was a gusher greater than any oil discovery. I simply had no control over The Balls. The more they pumped the more I kept spewing, the glistening white strands stretching from dick tip to shoulders. It was a jizz-fest like I'd never been part of before. Jason was writhing in uncontrollable pleasure thus flicking me and my ejaculating contents in all directions. The sheets were a cum covered mess.

I glanced up, and Mistress was capturing my finest moment on camera. For the first time, a smile radiated from her face indicating a great sense of satisfaction for her superb dominatrix work on this innocent lad - and I'm thinking, also on me.

She put down the camera and those red venomous lips came straight to me. She intended to enjoy the remains of the day, my delicious delayed dollops that invariably ooze out somewhat after the main action. She flicked her tongue all around my head before completely encompassing my now more sensitive head.

Jason, quite simply, couldn't cope with this additional sadistic act of gratitude. Simultaneously he screamed in tortured agony over her unrelenting pleasuring and ground his butt deeply into the sheets in a fruitless endeavor to escape her wickedness. His legs began to flail around wildly in all directions in a further effort to escape. As for me, my sensitivity was returning and I delighted in her warm mouth and tonguing abilities.

After receiving the last of my creamy offerings, she rose from me, took hold of the crop, placed it firmly under his chin and said

"You didn't say, Mistress..." - and having said that, she placed her cum-drenched lips on his, giving him a full measure of his own sweet creamy jizz deep into his mouth.

He was now totally hers in body, mind, and pleasure.

That certainly was a raunchy night - and a personal best performance, I'll never forget - and what's more, I've got the video to prove it!

PETER BENN

You can ooze charm for about 15 minutes.

After that, you'd better have a big dick!

PETER BENN

CHAPTER TWELVE

NUDE BEACH

There's nothing better than a raunchy day out at the nude beach. I get to hang out without clothing hindering my view, so I get to see it all just like you do. For a guy like me who is so often hidden away until the last minute, that's a treat.

On those days, there's a special bond between Jason and myself. It's almost like a direct connection between his eyes, his brain and me. Any of the three of us can alert the others to a potentially horny possibility. Jason can be standing chatting with a nice young woman while I'm dangling semi-erect right at the coal-face (so to speak). Without being too crass about it, he has trained me to send a message to him to let him know that everything is ready down below for imminent action and that what he is unable to see with his own eyes is in position for our entry. I know he has received my message when there's a subtle muscle spasm at the base of my shaft. I'm alert and ready, and now he can confidently continue the seduction of his new friend.

But I'm getting a bit ahead of myself as we haven't even arrived at the beach as yet.

We'd headed down the freeway and after an hour or so turned off on to a very rural road that was obviously not a thoroughfare to anywhere except the isolated nude beach. The sun was shining, the music was playing loudly in the car, Jason was wearing his new T-shirt and loose fitting shorts. I'm was in repose and enjoying the feeling of freeballing rather than being packaged up in tight jocks. It was definitely shaping up to be a good day (nude girls willing) and this time, mercifully, without the agony that followed our last outing like this.

Both he and I will not quickly forget the aftermath of the scorching sun on me, his unprotected willy. How he could have been so stupid as to forget to take the sunscreen will forever remain a mystery. Naked all afternoon on the beach, the nice episode with two girls on our over-sized beach towel, the laughter, the drinking, the walk back to the car. And then - THE BURNING!!!!

I was red hot, and not in the nice hot sexual way. No, no, no - I was burned through what felt like several layers of my skin. My head was as bright as a tomato beckoning to be picked and eaten. My length was pink to red with nice white original skin showing between the folds. This was not my best look.

By the time we were back at the car he took pity on me and decided to drive without covering me up with clothing. Perhaps it was the screams of agony whenever he had me touch any of his clothing that decided him on that action. I could rest the sac and The Balls on the seat without too much discomfort, but to achieve that he had to drive with those legs wide apart. Touch my head, even lightly with his hairy legs, and he instantly knew that I was not a happy best friend. His shrieks were constant, his brain totally focused on not moving a muscle.

Mind you, his burnt shoulders and even worse burnt butt-cheeks also added immeasurably to his agony while driving. There are not that many positions he dared to move into as he knew that any movement, even the tiniest, was like driving a million hot needles into that part of the skin. The air conditioning blasted cold air directly onto me and into the car. A bottle of water which was still cold and semi-frozen sat atop me trying to cool my skin. But nothing really worked. It was over an hour's drive home and it was going to be the longest, most painful hour for the both of us.

It was one of the very few times since we originally discovered beating off that any thought of sex of any kind was definitely off the immediate agenda for the both of us. A burnt willy knows exactly how to tell its owner that he is not happy. Sending constant messages of pain certainly focusses the owner's attention. The respect for me that followed was admittedly brief, but at least for a short time, I was well looked after.

The nurses at the Emergency Room of the hospital were also respectful of my agonized condition. I realized that when they laughed out loud it was not disrespectful towards me, but rather it was the failings of the male gender to properly look after their greatest asset. A woman's respect for her body would never allow this to happen to her extremities. So, when they gently held me and admired me, I could sense his embarrassment. They spoke kindly towards me as they slowly massaged the nurturing cream along my tender shaft and with their palm they gently circled my head knowing full well that a rub in the wrong direction might cause much pain to Jason. So, what if his agonized cry of "FAAAARRK" more than once echoed across the ER treatment area from the furthest cubicle. Those nurses were on my side and gave a lesson to my owner that he wouldn't quickly forget.

Even as we walked out of the hospital the agony was great. Bent over like an old man, legs wide apart, wearing the loosest possible fitting shorts, Jason looked a pale shadow of his youthful years.

"Been in the wars, have you mate?" said a would-be helpful patient-in-waiting. "Geeze, did you hear the cries of the guy in the far cubicle. Sounded like a hot poker was being thrust up his backside. I wouldn't want to be him for anything."

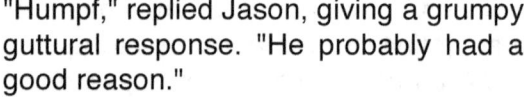

"Humpf," replied Jason, giving a grumpy guttural response. "He probably had a good reason."

"I know what it's like. I've had a couple of things pulled out of me in that area over the years...."

"Oh spare me," said Jason as he thought to himself "if ONLY it was a hot poker. If this guy really knew the agony I'm actually in ......"

Ten days without so much as a wank, let alone having full-on sex, allowed me to fully recover. Jason was dutiful in looking after me with creams several times a day. Sleeping all night on his back was a novelty for him that took quite a bit of getting used to especially on the first few nights when his shoulders also gave him angst.

During those first few days, I enjoyed testing his mettle as he knew that to have an erection would be painful. His eyes looked at passing women, his porn collection was obvious around the apartment, the distractions and sexual stimuli were everywhere. It didn't take much of a twitch from me to attract his attention. As the blood began to flow, so his eyes began to water, and his mind went into an "I-don't-want-to-know" phase. He tried to appease me by reverting his thinking to anything non-sexual. He couldn't take a cold shower as the agony of the falling water was like drumming on tender skin.

My favorite was when he opened the refrigerator door, dropped his shorts and stood there naked to the cold emanating from the inside. It was as close to a cold shower that he could think of.

But all of that is now a distant memory, a new summer season has come around and the nude beach beckoned once more...

We walked around the corner of the bluff situated at the end of the "family" beach and voila - there was our mixed-beach, naked destination just up ahead. Even further along in the distance was the gay enclave where nude men could be seen parading along the waterline advertising their special endowments to their all-male audience.

He, who must be obeyed, was delighted at the numbers there at the mixed beach that day. Various small groups of women, both young and old, male/female couples and a wide diversity of single men and an occasional single woman, could be seen. As he stripped off his shorts and T-shirt in order to make his grand, nonchalant naked entrance, I too got my first look at the visual delights on offer. While he looked at and sized up the faces and bodies, I only had my eye on their lower regions. And man, oh man, shaved genitalia were certainly de rigor that season - even for many of the men. I just didn't know where to look next!

PETER BENN

Oh, YES I did! The couple high up the beach near the trees were already well advanced in their afternoon lovemaking. Towels were spread, as were the legs. And there was a ready audience of grateful men admiring the antics while they stroked their own best friend. The afternoon was obviously going to be as raunchy as it was on our last visit.

With a casual stroll along the water's edge (the must-do, catwalk pose that anonymously announces the arrival of the latest sexual hopeful) Jason showed off both his muscles and my indisputable big size and good looks, for all to admire.

You could see how practically everyone on the beach had positioned themselves to get the best view of who else was there. Eyes slowly watched us from behind innocuous sunglasses, their heads moving slowly as they tracked our entrance, their minds deciding what the potential of Jason and myself might be for activities later in the afternoon or evening. I think that we are all voyeurs at heart, and just love to quietly be part of a nude/sexual scene where we can let our fantasies take flight. In reality, if anything does occur that we can be part of, well, that's a bonus. Everyone was at the beach that day to, in some way, further their sexual boundaries, enjoy the freedom of being close to nature and being free of clothing and/or to be part of a like-minded community.

With another casual drift, this time to the right, we started up the beach to find ourselves a patch of sand where we too, could position ourselves to make the most of the viewing and chatting opportunities. Jason decided on the area of pure white sand high up and not too far from the trees where our copulating couple was now finishing off. My master is an old hand at knowing the best places for sex. From the location he chose, we could watch those cruising through the trees, see the sex that takes place higher up in the upper circle of the beach rather than down among those purely here for sun-worshipping, and generally have a grand sweep of the beach to view anything that might happen and/or check-out all the new arrivals.

Slop! Slap! - and slop some more. I was covered in sunscreen. Indeed, those memories of sunburn I was telling you about were definitely NOT going to happen again this visit. No! No! NO!

As I peered out through the white cream mist of factor 30+ I could see he had positioned us superbly.

"May I..." he said to one of the three young women sharing two huge beach blankets. He offered his bottle of sunscreen and his open hand to her, and she agreed

"That would be nice. Thank you."

As his hands spread the cooling white cream across her shoulders, she laughed at the tickling feeling before then beginning to murmur that sound of contented submission Jason so expertly brings out in his women. I know from personal experience how intoxicating his hands can be on naked flesh, but this girl was smitten from the first cool palm stroke.

"You do that so divinely" she muttered. "When you finish my shoulders would you mind doing my breasts as well...."

By then I knew I was on immediate standby for a complete erection. Breasts, suntan cream, sex lubricant, my twitches and Jason's imagination were on a collision course that would DEFINITELY involve me being shown off to my best advantage.

"Lie back and let me do that for you," he said in his best bedside manner voice. "Close your eyes..."

And with that he was quickly on his knees beside her, doing his duty. As he gently moved his large hands across her well-proportioned assets my internal blood pump was set in motion. In no time, I had a higher viewpoint of her navel and breasts than I had a few seconds before. His hands continued to swirl and massage the cream into her flesh. Then, with his palms, he gently circled the nipples adding a tantalizing degree of stimulating friction.

Thwack!!!! Her hand accidentally knocked me.

"Fuck. What's that", she exclaimed, opening her eyes and looking down at me recoiling from the unexpected gesture.

"Jeez, I wasn't expecting THAT size!"

The other two girls sharing the blankets glanced over to see what the friend's fuss was all about.

Glancing at one another they gave approving nods to what their eyes were seeing. In my semi-dazed state, I took that as a double approval and continued quietly thinking to myself that indeed I am a fine up-standing asset to womankind.

While Jason remained on his knees holding the tube of suntan cream in one hand and the ready-to-spread cream in the other, she slid down the blanket to where her mouth came into full contact with me. I was plunged into total darkness. It felt good - very good! Then I saw sunshine again, then more total darkness. This continued for some time and obviously, she had no issues with the taste of my sun cream covering. I had the feeling that Jason was in a helpless position, what with his hands full and his knees buried in the warm sand, but I know him well enough to guess that he wasn't the least bit concerned.

This girl had obviously not eaten in a while as she was extraordinarily hungry and also needed to catch up on her oral exercise regime. Such enthusiasm for me as her new gym partner was to be commended. I knew my duty and I stayed rigid to the end, no matter how enthusiastic her tongue exercises became. It wasn't too long before I heard the words "Fuck I'm cumming" uttered by Jason. Suddenly I was blinded again by the summer sun just as I gave forth my gifts right across her breasts.

I normally hear words to the effect of "that was fantastic" or "OMG look at that load" but no, this time I heard applause. The two admiring female onlookers were all smiles and laughter as they clapped the outcome.

"I'll wash you off at the water" my master gallantly offered.

"No need" she smilingly replied, "I'll spread it around and let it dry for the moment. Then wash off later."

Perhaps this was some kind of symbol she wanted to enjoy and boast about. Whatever!

Anyway, we had serious sun-worshipping to undertake before going back on the prowl for interesting sex.

So, with another slop and slap, I was again covered in

sunscreen before lying limply naked to the burning sun with the inevitable seagulls circling overhead admiring the view and wishing that the smorgasbord of male sausage on display could be theirs to enjoy.

But for now, it was time to rest and top up the tan.

After a brief series of rotisserie turns where I was alternatively baked by the sun and then pushed headfirst into the towel and the sand underneath, Jason began a new survey of the sexual potential offered by the females on the beach.

As you know, there is a real art in hiding behind sunglasses while adroitly and surreptitiously surveying the world around you. When The Boss raised himself onto his elbow it also gave me a good view of the talent. In our relationship, I was seen as the carrot to be used to attract attention and consequently lure in impressed young women. We seemed to have the greatest success when I was a little larger than slack, maybe as big as a semi-erection but not so large as to frighten the timid or the inexperienced when it came to handling an appendage my size.

And so, it was, that the message came down to harden up a little and let's start displaying the wares. It was Showtime!

The area we were sitting in comprised a number of male/female couples sitting/lying on the sand and behind us was a wooded thicket area with tracks running through it. Most of the beach visitors seemed to be there for the sun and not for the sex, though over on the right a small group of mostly men, were standing around a couple who were obviously having sex and enjoying being the center of interest for the masturbating voyeurs.

One of the standing group had his cell phone in one hand videoing the activities, while the other hand was busy jerking off.

No chance of us getting involved there. It was, therefore, the tracks that interested Jason as he observed there was a steady stream of naked men and women using them. Some had a towel nonchalantly thrown over a shoulder, others carried a lube tube, a few of the women had panties on but still remained bare-breasted, but all were looking for some indication of sexual interest from others. There were single men, some of whom Jason suspected would continue to walk further along to the farthest end of the beach where the gay guys were doing the same trolling for sex as was happening where we were. Here there were straight and bi couples, though very few single women took to the track.

Not long after observing all this, The Boss decided it was time to investigate the secrets of what was happening beyond the prying eyes on the beach. It began with a ritual of course. The slow standing up, the languid brushing of sand off his body, the seemingly inconsequential re-adjustment of me and The Balls into the best position - (we only have ONE position anyway but it does draw attention to us for anyone who happens to be looking) - the sunglasses adjusted back onto the face, the fingers pushed backwards through the hair. Indeed, The Boss needs to always feel that he looks "cool" before going on Pussy Patrol.

We stood for a moment like a god surveying all the nakedness before us, and with no immediate response from the nearby couple, we walked up to and onto the sandy track, taking the track to the right just behind two men and a woman who seemed to be very at ease with one another. In the heat of the afternoon, the wooded area was hot and still, almost without any breeze and with the sound of the hidden insect life creating a low-level hum, especially from the cicadas as they sent out their own monotonous mating chorus. It was a very different atmosphere to the beach. Here and there the track passed the edge of the beach where those in the know had discovered almost hidden sandy depressions where they sunbaked, chatted with friends, slowly masturbated, fucked or simply watched the naked trolling walkers pass by.

I was in semi-erection all the time as Jason's eyes could hardly contain themselves as they birthed new fantasies with every breast and every vagina that walked towards us. I was transfixed as it's not often that I get the same opportunity to view the world as my man does. Naturally, I was also comparing myself to the guys that passed us. Not that I'm insecure about my size or abilities, but I do have an ego and I do like to know that I'm better than average - MUCH better than average - in length and girth. Being reassured by that I can then do my utmost to make sure that both Jason and his lady friend have the best possible experience.

I was quietly contemplating the passing lengths, widths, shaved, unshaved, muscle-bound, skinny, fat, bleached, sunburnt and deliciously desirable men and women when we turned a corner to find a full-on orgy group happening.

There must have been a least a dozen towels spread out across the sparse grassy vegetation that formed into one large blanket, and there was equally that number in various states of fucking, sucking or masturbating. It was just what Jason had been hoping for to give us a memorable afternoon's activity.

There is, of course, etiquette about joining in. One doesn't plunge into activity without some form of invitation, whether that be a smile or a beckoning finger. Jason and I quietly moved to the edge of the toweled area and stood there looking at the scene. All ages were represented, though perhaps with a bias toward the more mature age group. As Jason had observed at other sexual events, the more mature players were without a doubt, some of the horniest people on the planet. They accepted whatever age had done to their body and simply got on with their pursuit of sexual pleasure, no matter who was watching. I've noticed that as Jason has aged, he too, has become more relaxed and accepting of his body, though sometimes he's still a little shy about having others watch me go through my paces when I'm pumping hard. Showing me off and pulling a sexy woman to him is no problem; it's just that when he's made the catch, he's keen to make the following activities a more private intimate affair. As for me, I'm happy letting anyone watch. I know my worth in a sexual situation, so as they say "if you've got IT, flaunt IT".

We watched the activity, all the while eager to join in, just waiting for a nod of approval from someone in the group. With a gentle full-shaft stroke or two, I was fluffed up in order to strut my stuff. With my engorged package now enticingly on display (did someone compare me to a peacock with his tail feathers upright and displaying all his finery), it didn't take long before the Fickle Finger of Fabulousness beckoned us over.

She was mid-thirties, with gym-toned, tight breasts, and a shaved pussy - all those things that The Boss thought about as we worked out in our gym. The man she was with was sensually caressing her and looked similarly toned, a decade older, hairless, obviously very proud of his trophy woman. As we walked the few steps to where they were, I immediately noticed that she was already on her knees, perfectly positioned at my height, with her engorged red lips waiting for my arrival.

In no time, the lights went out for me and I was once again fulfilling the fantasy and desire of another very attractive woman. MMMMmmmm it felt so good being in there away from the hot sun. She didn't even notice the residue of the suntan cream on my length and head. But then, perhaps she did, for she cleaned both my length and head with a tongue that was as enthusiastic as any that we have encountered. Oh, YES, Ma'am, MMMMmmmm...

She indicated that she wanted to move onto her back so that I could enter her mouth while her enthusiastic and horny partner ate her out down below. Jason straddled her, feeling her tight nipples press tantalizingly against The Buns. As he leaned forward I returned to her mouth. She soon realized as I tried to go deep into the back of her throat, that from that angle she could only take part of me. It's surprising that a noisy gag reflex always turns heads on those who might otherwise be oblivious to what was happening near them. As I was quickly pulled out I could see others in various states of *flagrante delicto* curiously wondering what the fuss was about. Once they saw me and what she was attempting to fill her mouth and throat with, they nodded their approval, smiled in envy or agreement, and simply carried on. They instinctively knew that I was a special treat, that there was needed a certain mastery of the oral delights of life to be able to manage and enjoy me. No doubt if they hadn't otherwise been fully occupied at the time, they would have happily exchanged places and received that satisfaction I could so obviously give them.

I was moved back into her mouth but with my length restrained. Soon, she was murmuring sweet sounds, not only from the ecstasy of having me pump her mouth but also from the stimulating in/out action now being provided by her gourmet-eating beach partner and his enthusiastic dick.

I was delighted to be given so much attention, and this continued for what seemed a considerable amount of time. In due course, I started to feel those first pangs of potential discharge so I was removed and taken to the now empty lower reaches for a change of scenery. With her legs over Jason's shoulders, into her now supple, moist – nay, wet – sloppy-second depths I was plunged. This time there was no gag-like struggle sounds as my full length reached deep into her body. Her reaction was one impassioned, muffled but very satisfying "MMMMMmmmmmmm" - and if I read that rightly, that response seemed to silently cry out "Fuck, you are a big boy aren't you... but I love it". Well, what could I do but blush in obvious silent agreement – and give her an extra strong twitch in gratitude?

Her partner by this stage, was on his knees beside her head, dipping his uncut dick complete with her pussy juices, into her well-rehearsed and enthusiastic mouth. Jason's messages to me indicated his approval of watching her take the other guy's hot dick. Each of the men had one hand on one of her breasts. With gentleness, The Boss leaned forward, mid-stroke, and began licking the pink nipple he'd been kneading. The messages quickened apace with that and soon, the inevitable series of "cumming soon" directions were issued as the immediate top priority for Jason and myself.

"Cum in her," said the partner. "Give her a cream-pie so that I can get my rocks off eating her out".

There was no time to do otherwise. Like the pressure in a blocked hose that's finally being released, I deluged into her depths, shot after shot after shot. Oh, it was such a relief to get rid of that second load of the afternoon.

And when I emerged back into the daylight, everyone seemed exceedingly happy about the foregoing proceedings and in particular, my performance. Jason and I had achieved our afternoon goal, Gym Lady had achieved a minor orgasm and now her partner, while masturbating himself, began the joy of eating my creamy deposit as it languidly oozed from her body. It seemed that everybody was happy.

And with my juices spent, (at least for the time being), Jason and I returned to the sun-drenched world of the beach, where all of its inhabitants were blissfully oblivious to the sexual debauchery taking place just a bit up the track behind them. Down in the shallows, with its gentle lapping waves, Jason washed me off and then for good hygiene sake, took a long leak into the water. That cleaned me out of any possible infection from the barebacking raw sex and we returned to the towel for another suntan top-up.

As we soaked up the late afternoon sun we both dreamed of even more sexual adventures together knowing that as Team Jason, we were the best of buddies and that single life was "absolutely, one hundred percent and without a doubt" one glorious, permanent, on-going and debauched sex party.

What else did we need to be happy?

Warning: Condoms do not guarantee safe sex.

A friend of mine was wearing one when he was shot by the woman's husband.

PETER BENN

CHAPTER THIRTEEN

THE BI-CURIOUS TRACK JOCK

Jason has always enjoyed sport, particularly as sport to him means exercise, fitness, good health. Double that up with a gym exercise program and that meant muscle. And muscle meant attracting admiring women - and men!

Yes, Jason was keenly aware that he had both the good looks and the body, both of which enabled him to pull a date whenever he wanted or needed one. I was also incorporated into that image of his muscled sexuality. He wasn't backward in using me to help advertise his sexual attractiveness to the opposite sex. My length, girth, and immediate availability were often the deciders as to which lucky girl was the one who was going to be in for a treat.

I was generally "dressed to the left" so that my considerable attributes pointedly hung down his leg on obvious display - and when erect, and especially when in tight clothing, I was more than obvious. I offered exciting potential to any imaginative female who discovered and looked upon my bulging "lunch" status as highly desirable. As you know, "it pays to advertise" was one expression he used, as was "if you've got it, flaunt it". Both worked equally well for us.

Jason played many sports over the years of his teenage and early adult life. I've been squeezed into tight-fitting stretch fabric for his gymnastics period, scrunched into a jock strap for the soccer, pushed under between his legs for his swim meets (he didn't want me to embarrass him with a woody while on the starting blocks) and hung free in the voluminous board shorts he wore for surfing.

During that intense sporting period, I certainly got around and experienced just about every twist and turn that a human penis is capable of having thrust upon it. And yes, I was even sidelined on one occasion when a heavy boot collided with me rather than on the football we were chasing.

Oh, fuck, did that hurt!

And not only at the time it happened but also when the bruising came up. The Balls didn't escape either and in fact, they had a worse time of it than I did. Bruising down there is very uncomfortable and takes longer to heal than elsewhere. But I did have to laugh when I saw how black they looked. When you've only ever seen them hairy and white then to see them velvet black with a bit of red rash is a shock. They were certainly not amused as I dangled there, one eye on them, day after day during the healing process, not-so-quietly chuckling away to myself. The bruising also caused all sorts of agony to The Boss. No tight jocks for a couple of weeks, lots of time spent in the bath letting me and The Balls float around thus giving him some much-needed instant relief from the pain. Sitting down to eat or watching television was an exercise in stealth as he s-l-o-w-l-y slipped delicately into a position where myself and the dingleberries caused no additional consternation, almost as if he was trying to ignore our delicate situation.

And dare I mention the bathroom visits? Freedom from clothing did give him much relief, but to even touch me in order to give me the direction to pee was agony beyond belief for him. You've read that men and pain are a lethal combination - and especially with all those "I'm going to die" stories when struck down by the common cold or flu. Well, they drift into insignificance with dick and ball bruising. Childbirth and kidney stones are high on the pain threshold list, but undressing and trying to pee when bruised is by any man's terms, THE most agonizing trial of all. During this time my inside tubes were somewhat tender, and when a hot stream under pressure comes tumbling through you didn't have to wait long for the screams of "Oh, fuck, F-A-R-KKKKK!". The neighbors, though somewhat used to Jason's triumphant outbursts when I shoot his load, were, during this period of bruise recovery, no doubt astonished at the perceived increased severity of the orgasm - and the frequency - morning, noon AND night. Little did they know that there were no women whatsoever in our bedroom and nor would there be for some time to come (if you pardon my expression). This was a period of pain and endurance that was right up there with the worst symptoms of the flu!

Jason and I also enjoyed the camaraderie that existed in the showers after a big game or a gym workout. As I have already expressed, he and I were not averse to nudity and showing ourselves off to the other guys as they flicked towels at naked butts, made obscene jokes about bending over and picking up the dropped soap and generally expressing their masculinity in whatever form of rough and tumble they thought appropriate at the time. It was also a time to compare the chiseled muscle results from all those hours spent in the gym.

And though it was rarely directly spoken of, comparison of dick sizes was also on everyone's agenda. Whether that meant trying to mentally position yourself in the hierarchy of team members as to where your own size placed you, or just allocating yourself into Team Cut or Team Uncut, everyone surreptitiously spied on everyone else. Jason was always proud of me and my size. By implication, that meant he was always highly regarded in the sexual ability stakes. In the mind of athletic jocks, a big dick always equals highly sexed and therefore always a hit with the girls.

I too looked around at my fellow penises and made comparisons. I have to admit that I can hold my head high when it comes to where I am in the size stakes. I've no curves to the left or the right, no discernible difference in coloring between my head and my shaft, no hood to hide my good looks under, no arched shaft that constantly looks downwards towards the floor - and I have pride in my strong muscle co-ordination that can be instantly activated with little more than a flicker of The Boss's eyes. My length is considerable and my head hangs well beyond the ball sac. Jason vacillates between shaven, trimmed and au naturel, but at this particular point of my working life, my naturally occurring bushy surroundings were being regularly trimmed so that meant I also looked a bit larger than my natural state might imply. Jason's washboard flat stomach also helped in this regard. He has always been pleased with my appearance and particularly with my never-fail performance.

The stories we have heard about sexual infections, brewer's droop and unhygienic quickies told us that we are a good team and way above the average in all things sexual. We don't take *too* many risks with me riding raw. Sure, alcohol tends to blind our instinct to reduce that risk by using condoms (often there are no condoms anyway) and after all, she's probably on The Pill – or should be. Hence we are always up for the next Fanny Boo opportunity with me preferably, riding bareback.

But all this locker-room bravado and gesticulating can also work the other way, with men admiring other men in a same-sex attracted way.

Kyle was top honcho in the athletics track and field team. He quite simply could run faster than anyone else we knew. Therefore, he constantly won his events at the track meets and as winners are grinners, he was subsequently one of the most popular dudes in college. The faculty loved the prestige his wins bought the college, his team-mates enjoyed basking in his success, and the females just couldn't get enough of his body. His success with women was legendary, awesome in fact. His ultra-fit body, his chiseled muscles, his strong legs, the considerable bulge under his track shorts, all contributed to him being a chick magnet. Jason and I enjoyed being on the team and especially the winning celebrations. There was always plenty of alcohol at these events, lots of outrageous behavior and more than enough eager honey-pots for the guys to choose from for later in the night. Kyle's Cast-Offs (as his extraneous girls were described by his teammates) were always very welcome and as track groupies, none of them went home to sleep alone. Jason and I enjoyed many a night with multiple young ladies sharing a bed or two with several of us young athletes.

Even so, it was a surprise when Kyle invited Jason and

me to share a threesome with him and his best friend Carley over at his apartment on a week-night.

Jason and I had long admired Kyle's physical attributes as he soaped himself under the shower after his workout. His dedication to physical fitness was extraordinary and it showed in every inch of his body. And his appendage was, not to put too fine a point on it, even bigger than I am. Uncut, thicker and a bit longer. Yeah, he's uncut and proud of it. One of the few guys on the team still intact, he was frequently being singled out for attention and the butt-end of dick jokes.

I was most impressed, and particularly delighted when his penis shared amazing stories with me and the other penis guys of what he and Kyle enjoyed together. About the eye-popping reactions from the girls when first seeing the length and width of the monster that they were about to try to cover with their mouth and then feel inside them. And with even more startled looks when they saw the hood still covering the delights waiting inside.

"Awe fuck – you've still got your hoodie – you didn't tell me that, you creep. How in the fuck am I supposed to suck and fuck that!!! I only fuck cut guys, real guys... I hate cheese." Oh, yes, bias was alive and well when it came to the feminine appreciation of what was widely considered a "proper" John Thomas.

Fortunately, such bias towards hoods and cock-cheese were not issues that I had to usually cope with. I'll admit that Jason's three-day camping trip to the mountains a couple of summers ago where we went without bathing for the whole time, would have had cheesy repercussions if we had had any chance of bedding a girl. As that opportunity wasn't to be, we survived and quickly got back into our daily ablution routine as soon as we got back home. Mind you, the atmospheric ripeness of four very smelly guys confined in a small car for the three-hour trip home was something I wouldn't quickly want to share again anytime soon! Some of that was just body odor, but as I well knew from my own pungent head corona, cock-cheese was rampant on each of them and as with all ripe cheeses, there was a special piquant that marked its territorial strength. No girl – or guy – would have found any of the four of us anything other than obnoxious that night.

But back to the adventures of Kyle and the Uncut Kid...

As Kyle's cock continued to speak, I devoured his every word, every nuance. About his highly evocative one-eyed descriptions of the struggle to inch-by-inch, press his way into tight crevices, often where no man or penis had been before - "just like squeezing into a standard condom when only "Giant Size" will do". Of having to deflower yet another virgin and his consequent struggle to tear asunder the natural barriers that Mother Nature uses to keep out undesirable impetuous male youth like his master – "like head-butting cling-wrap stretched across a cave entrance" was one colorful description he provided. Deflowering virgin girls was Kyle's top sexual priority.

"Fark, it's messy" he would often say when holding court with the other jocks, "but I'll be the one she'll always remember, you can be sure of that. For the rest of her life, every other dude in there will be silently judged against my size and performance. You just can't beat being the first!"

I'd also observed Kyle's glances in my direction as Jason soaped me, washed me and dried me in the adjacent shower. I could tell that he was still pleased that his schlong was bigger, yet he was suitably impressed that I was a genuine threat to his being the biggest meat sword in the team. Over the months, no words were spoken by either Kyle or Jason about their appendages, not even the differences between cut and uncut, but I could tell that there was genuine silent respect moving both directions between the boys.

"Carley likes big dick and yours is the biggest I know of other than mine, so how's about it? She's hot man and wants to do a DP. You up for it? Tuesday, 7.30 my place."

"Shit, yeah" was the immediate answer from upstairs.

"All raw. No condoms. Just pull out and cream her face. She loves that."

The scene for the evening had been set, and we arrived just before the start time. Jason knew Carley from watching her indulge at other group sex nights, but I hadn't had the opportunity to share with her my meaty delights. So, there was more than a passing interest in having me work my wonders into this girl.

How Jason would respond to sharing nudity and an intimate sex scene with another guy was something high in my thoughts. He had coped ok at the occasional drunken orgy with his other team and college mates, though he seemed to always just want the girl all to himself. Would this be any different?

The drinks flowed freely, beginning with two lots of shots all around, and then beer for the boys and a mixed cocktail for her.

It didn't take too long for the action to get underway - the kissing, the groping, the rapid removal of clothing. I was excited and I could see that my brother-in-arms was also no longer hanging down from Kyle but rather standing to full attention. Carley was using her mouth to bring the two dicks together, firstly using her dexterous mouth on Kyle Cock and then down on to me. It was a struggle even with her enthusiastic mouth, but she managed the both of us - well, our heads, at least - into her mouth. Up close and intimate with my compatriot we compared notes, knowing that we were both going to have a great night.

"Kyle and I will take her pussy and you can fuck her butt," he said to me. "That's what Mr. K has in mind."

"I've had no message to that effect" I chokingly replied. "The Boss says that it will be an all pussy affair - one of us underneath, the other from behind."

"Look, man, I've been in there so many times and there's simply no room for the both us without splitting the poor girl from afternoon to breakfast."

However, I wasn't going to admit that one of her orifices was as good as another as far as I was concerned. Yeah, cleanliness can be an issue in the back entrance, but as Jason says, "Shit happens. Get over it". Wet vagina adventures were, of course, my favorite mode of pleasuring but when ye oldie period was an issue or that fear of pregnancy raised its ugly possibility, then back-door trekking had a practical and still pleasurable outcome.

"Then pull your head into your hood and face facts - we're both going to share giving her exactly what she wants. She wants and she'll get, TWO dicks, in the same place at the same time. Comprendez? You might be fat and fill up most of her, but I've been known to slip into some very tight situations and the girl has never been disappointed. Our Bosses will get her wet and lube her up, and then I'm in there too."

You could tell from the tightening of his skin that he was not used to being spoken to like this. He'd been King Dick too long and as such dictated the course of events. Well, he'd met his match this day.

"And of course you realize that after Carley leaves, Kyle wants you to ride him deep within his butt too...."

"What.... WHAT!!!!!!" I screamed.

I very nearly prematurely heaved out a load into the girl's mouth I was so surprised and taken aback. I'd been totally and unexpectedly gazumped by this thick prick I was sharing a moment with.

And won't Jason be totally taken by surprise, I immediately thought to myself. This turn of events would have to be the furthest thought from his ever-lovin' heterosexual butch macho and coochie-chasing image. Sure, we'd both admired Kyle under the showers for his body and yes, dare I admit it - his big donger, but to go blindly into the backroads of buggery with him was a thought not yet within a light-year of being thought of - by either of us. The Boss is more than happy to share friendships and social fun times with several other gay athletes, but he hasn't expressed to me any thoughts of wanting to go to bed with any of them.

OK, ok, yes, to be honest, there has been an envious twitch or two sent down to me at various times when a nice dick or male butt is expressing itself in some show-off way. Jason admires the physicality of human beauty of all kinds, both female and to a lesser extent, the male. But other than those occasional twitches - nothing.

Alright, alright - I know you can read between the lines in what I'm saying. Yes, yes, yes - the guys in the straight threesomes and moresomes porn videos can be very attractive for Jason to watch in action, but he justifies this as being educative, a visual form of learning how to be a better lover. It's not about lust, though I do get a beating EVERY time he watches a DVD or porn channel "sexual classroom" but it's more about a teacher/student relationship where the demonstration is about putting theory into practice.

He likes to imagine that he and I are in the position of the active guy with the girl in the video. As a result, his head is filled with sexual fantasy which gets immediately transmitted down to me and I then have to perform. As a bonus, while his hand is pumping me I get to watch the on-screen action too, and that stirs me to a better performance every time. My emptying of The Balls is always enhanced when I'm stimulated by what I see and what hand is upon me, just as much as when The Boss sends down his own directions.

But if tonight plays out the way Kyle's Uncut Kid tells it, then it will be one to remember.

"Just curious. Just sexually experimenting. Just .... don't tell anyone!" Mmmm, I can already hear the logic and the justification....

The evening progressed as anticipated with lots of M/M/F and M/F touching and kissing and oral expression - and unexpectedly, much more M/M touch and pleasuring than Jason initially expected.

"Oh, well, it's all part of having a threesome" he justified silently to himself. "We're both here to make HER happy. Nothing gay in that."

When it came to that double penetration, I have to admit that my size, when added to that of the Uncut Kid's bulk, was too much for Carley to cope with. Our two owners did try very enthusiastically to both penetrate us Wang Doodles into her Pickle Jar at the same time, but it just wasn't going to be successful.

Kyle lay on his back with the Uncut Kid pointing straight up so that Carley could sit on it while looking down at the owner. Our role was to come from behind while Carley bent forward to nibble Kyles' nipples. Loads of lube was fingered into her and doused all over me. From where I was coming from I could see an opening happening that grew bigger as she leaned forward. As I was free of any restrictive latex clothing, the lube would certainly allow me to merge in alongside Kyle's dick and then slip deep inside, pushing and sliding as I pressed against the other shaft.

Jason lined me up and aimed me right into the open crevice from where I was to make my assault. With a gentle push from The Boss, I plunged into the warm, slippery darkness. I'd barely entered when I was rudely squeezed tight between the other shaft and a not-so-pliable-any-more Twinkle Cave wall. Carley had bucked backward in reaction to my arrival. She screamed - and not from delight. Her body tightened and her pelvic walls stopped any further advance of my manhood.

"Pull out! Pull out!" she shouted. And as quickly as a hot knife slices through butter I was seeing the bedroom lighting again. I could see that she was very happily being filled to near capacity by my opposition, so I was repositioned to stand over her and be lined up with her lips in readiness for a blow job. And then it happened...

"Fuck, I can't hold back" Kyle cried as he began pumping deep into Carley's pleasure zone. "I'm cumming, I'm cumming...."

I hadn't even reached her lips before I was denied any oral action. Jason, and sadly, I too, had to retreat.

"Fuck, you came in me" she shouted. "You bastard..."

In the blink of an eye, she was off him and into the bathroom to empty herself.

"Pull up a pillow bro," said Kyle still lying with his back on the bed trying to get his normal breathing back.

In a short time, Carley emerged fully dressed and still furious....

"I'm leaving! You two have fun fucking each other, but I'm off ... finished." and she stormed off, slamming the apartment door behind her.

"And what did she mean by that" questioned Jason.

"Aw Geez, bro, we'd both talked about you before we asked you for the threesome. And I happened to say that if anyone was going to get me to show my bi side then that dude would be you...." - and he placed his hand on Jason's nipple.

I immediately flinched back to erection, whether that be because of Jason's direct link from nipple to me, or the fact that it was an exciting, dangerous idea he'd just been presented with.

"You'd like to fuck with ME?" added Jason.

"Yeah bro, I think you're cool."

"And so are you. But ... to make it with you - we'd have to keep it just between ourselves... and tell absolutely no-one."

"Fuck yeah. I've got an image to maintain" added Kyle.

They'd both had had a lot to drink but there they were, lying naked, side by side on the bed. Jason knew that I'd need to get off one way or another before any attempt at sleep later that night. Therefore, the suggestion was not one to be ignored.

"If you touch the other one I'll get even harder" Jason seductively and quietly responded.

And with that, Kyle began playing with both The Boss's nipples, therefore sending me once more into waves of erectile pleasure. I was still so horny from the misadventures with Carley's Twinkle Cave that it didn't take more than a few nipple tweaks to get me really excited again. And when Kyle moved in and began to kiss my man, then the pleasure sensations moved into a higher gear. I was beginning to get really excited at the direction this new adventure was taking.

As they kissed more and more passionately, they rolled together so that once more the Uncut Kid and I were squashed together between the heaving bodies. There wasn't a lot of opportunity for talking as the demands of frottage kept us both on the go, up and down the two bodies. He had said that I'd be the one going in to do the work as being the passive recipient was exactly what

Kyle was looking for. It seems that he was tired of always being the active aggressor in all his sexual situations with women when really, all he wanted, was the chance to lie back, swing his legs into the air and be seduced and entered by a hard and enthusiastic dick. It seems that he did get pegged occasionally with a dildo strap-on that he would present to any particularly adventurous girl he could trust to keep her mouth shut about such things. Kyle had high hopes for himself that night, so a quiet douching before we arrived meant that he was clean and ever-hopeful for a bottoming session.

Not only was I getting a real workout between the two bodies, I was getting a unique sexual education about the variety of sex that can happen in the sanctity of sexual spaces. It was an eye-opener to learn that we should never take any sexual situation just at face value. People are always capable of a million variations if the circumstances are conducive to that possibility.

The Uncut Kid was erect like a lighthouse beaming out its location to a lost world. Jason had certainly noticed - and felt against his skin - the size and appeal of its possibilities. But then Kyle was feeling the same about Jason and me.

They obviously both wanted to know what the other's dick felt like in their mouth. Jason moved around the bed until the two of them were in a sixty-nine position, each with a stiff dick positioned ready for some oral action. I just had time to look along the washboard abs to see Jason roll back the skin package, take a big gulp and suck the now exposed Uncut Kid into his mouth. It WAS a big mouthful to cope with, so only the head had disappeared into warm flesh before I too was engulfed in darkness.

I was barely inside this warm oral man-cave when I simply had to scream out...

"Teeth. THE TEETH. THE T-E-E-E-E-T-H!!!!!!"

Oh, my giddy aunt, they were like razor wire against my sensitive skin.

Jason immediately pulled off of his meaty meal and passed on my urgent excruciating message to Kyle (who I had by then dubbed, Toothy Fang the Third) who was still all too oblivious to the potential injury and scarring he was inflicting let alone the pain that went with that. I'd had a number of girls who also had not practiced their craft on some docile cooked bratwurst or peeled banana as they should have before deciding to go for the real male thing. Bananas and cooked sausage might not respond to molesting molars or have pain thresh-holds – but I surely do!

On behalf of all of my fellow adult male appendages around the world - that's about two and a half billion of us (I know, I know, there's no shortage of dick available if you start looking) – but please, please, p-l-e-a-s-e, don't go down on any of us without having at least a modicum of experience in the art of teeth retraction. Nothing turns me off more quickly to giving you satisfaction than having a fang scrape along my shaft or an incisor touch my head and soft neckline. If that happens, then instantly I'm done in and it will take a lot of coaxing to get me back into love-making mode.

When the mood is punctured, it's a massive turnoff for us usually easy-going dick guys. I've talked to a few of the older more experienced dicks who hang around the change rooms and they say that you can't beat (pun intended) a mouth with the false teeth removed. Their opinion is that nothing beats a gummy experience as it lets the partner chow down on their favorite sausage for as long as they want. And that is always to OUR benefit as it delays the heaving until WE'RE ready to shoot. It's not happened to me yet, but I guess as I age the opportunity will arise.

Fortunately, in this instance, I was so turned-on by the novelty and curiosity of the situation, I was quickly back in the saddle (well, his mouth) and we proceeded from there as a mutually respectful duo. I did drop Kyle a few pearls of pre-cum just to encourage him and his taste buds to enjoy the experience. He needed to know that he was sucking off a professional dick that is used to being treated as such. He is a top athlete in his particular field of sport and in my own way, so am I. So, a little "thank you" juice is always appropriate for me to give at such times.

We continued in that sixty-nine position for several more minutes. It being relatively new to both the guys, there was consequently also a lot of laughter coming from the inexperience they both knew was behind the encounter. It was clear that this was simply a fun time, a satisfying of curiosity, a mutually agreeable inexperienced fuck-fumble that was as entertaining and educational as it was erotic and chaotic.

In due course, I again saw the light in the room - and I saw Jason reach for the lube and began to smear it around Kyle's Love Tunnel. Kyle responded, granting exclusive access by lifting his muscular legs onto Jason's shoulders. Directly ahead of me I could see the finger firstly rubbing the outside, then gingerly taking the opportunity to slip into forbidden territory.

Kyle was openly moaning with pleasure and grinding his

body deeper onto Jason's digit. With a thwack of lube thrust on to me - and along me, - I was on the move.

I WAS GOING IN!!!!!!!

AAAARRRGGGGHHHH!!!!!

Kyle was ready and prepared for Jason's "Wicked Wang" (aka as moi) to proceed.

Well, no, - he wasn't quite THAT prepared. I was barely in head-deep when I was unceremoniously withdrawn as Kyle reacted to a pain thresh-hold that he was obviously not ready to admit to.

"F-A-R-R-R-R-K!!!!!!! More lube, more lube..." I heard as an anguished, desperate cry from near the pillow.

This all-macho athletic jock was as vulnerable to the perceived yucky discomforts as any of us is to anal penetration of any kind - whether that be from a prostate check-up using a finger in a rear-end to a hot guy using his dick up a woman as a birth control method. Even the thought of a thermometer up the anal canal can bring tears to the eyes of some.

Now, here was I, not the smallest dick in the country, going into reasonably virginal territory where big digits, either the artificial dildo variety or the genuinely meaty reality, had rarely entered. Still, there was nothing I could do about it. I'm big, I'm proud. So - suck it up Jock Baby and let me do my job.

Jason must have received my message, so with additional lube all around, he wasn't going to waste much more time in opening up the flighty Kyle Hole.

BACK IN I WENT!   AAAARRRGGGGHHHH!!!!! for the second time.

Deeper, D-e-e-p-e-r, D-E-E-P-E-R!!!

Like a massive tunnel borer creating new underground train passages, I continued in right up to his sphincter muscle. Now, this needed a bit of extra effort from The Boss. Those tight walls narrowed my entry into the heavenly space beyond, so they had to be pushed back. As my head achieved that, not only was there a constricting body movement from a now non-virginal, deflowered Kyle that underscored a "believe me, dude, you're the only guy that's ever been in there" justification statement - but the muscle walls flapped back and gripped the corona behind my head with vice-like tension. It sure felt like an experienced tunnel operator to me!

I was in, and that meant a moment for Kyle to savor the relief from my aggression and my size before Jason began the age-old, in-out technique of mutual gratification. As I was finding out that night, whether I'm in a male or a female, it is all the same to me. Same technique, different pleasure zones to rub against me but much-the-same dark moist environment that will eventually make me heave. It turns out after all, that I'm not the least sexist or racist or ageist. If you're an adult - male or female - with an appreciation for friendly dick, then you and I should get to know one another much more intimately.

Jason began the movement of me by withdrawing and then thrusting. I could feel the vice-like grip relaxing, the well-lubricated channel now giving both myself and Kyle enormous pleasuring as I was withdrawn full shaft, then plunged balls-deep back into him.

Having not lost my load earlier in the night and now having sensational sex in a whole new erotic environment, I was not going to last. I communicated that upstairs and he understood. This wasn't a love tryst made in heaven. This was two young drunk guys sorting out and putting into practice their erotic dreams and wildest unspeakable fantasies. It was just like beating off but in this instance, they happened to use the Love Tube of the other instead of a hand or a mouth or one of those useful hold-in-the-hand artificial orifices.

And tomorrow on the track neither would acknowledge the intimate sexual adventures that took place the night before. That's what sexually adventurous straight men do. They quietly have the sex, but it is then locked away in the memory for use only when some artificial stimulation image is required to bring them to climax.

I was really getting so close to shooting. The blood was pumping into me, the pulse of my shaft was beating at a furious rate, The Balls had shouted out that "All Systems Are Go", and my outer lubed skin was so sensitive I couldn't take another single pass along Kyle's canal. I was set for my first-ever, fuck-a-guy-up-the-ass cream-pie climax. And let me tell you I didn't disappoint!

Even with my head buried deep beyond the sphincter walls I heard him scream simultaneously with my first projectile vomit. Wham! Right to the back of that heavenly valley it exploded. And right on cue, his body spasmed in response. I was as erotically charged as ever I had been, so the relief from that first blast simply opened up the floodgates of my creamy reservoirs.

Jason enthusiastically thrust me in and out a couple more times, before plunging me once more deep into the cream pool I had created. I was deep, deep, deep in my own hot splodge. My whole shaft pulsed and raced exactly like I would have done with Carley. I am never happier than wallowing in my own juice deep within a dark human cavern, so when Jason called "Time Out", it was with reluctance that I backed up along that slippery slope and saw the bed light again.

I was out just in time to witness Kyle wanking himself to climax and shooting his second load for the night. Oh, he was good. I'll admit that. That second load was impressive, which says a lot about Jason and I pushing him and The Uncut Kid to bigger and better end results. The whole atmosphere was very erotically charged and all four of us, both guys and both dicks, were in agreement that the outcome was exactly what we all wanted to achieve.

"Fuckin' hell. That was unreal," said Kyle as he looked up appreciatively to Jason. "That dick of yours felt so friggin' good, I could feel every inch of it. Thanks." and with that Kyle bent over me and gave me a kiss and a tongue lick. I swelled a little with renewed pride and oozed another bonus extra droplet for him to taste.

At that moment, I suspected that perhaps - just perhaps - neither Jason nor Kyle were as "straight" as the world perceived them.

But my dear reader, that's our dirty little secret to keep just between ourselves - just as they will keep it between themselves until late one very drunken night, when in a wild sense of bravado or one-upmanship, one or the other will spill the dirt about what REALLY happened...

PETER BENN

My dick is only 2 inches...

from the ground!

PETER BENN

CHAPTER FOURTEEN

THE FLUFFER

"It's just for one day. The pay is good and you might get to fuck the leading lady at the end of it all like I did" said Kyle to Jason. "That might mean sloppy seconds" he added, "But who cares when it's the gorgeous Trixie. Make sure that you're as horny as hell as it's all important that you can perform for the entire day. They don't like it when dicks droop."

"One hundred percent mate. That'd be awesome."

"Thursday morning, about nine, meet at Hung Lo Studios then it's off on location to some sumptuous mansion in the hills."

This was like satisfying Jason's most fantasy-fueled sexual dreams. And as a consequence - mine. I'd deposited in some fun places before that week, but never, to my knowledge, been offered one of the top female porn stars. Now THAT would be a treat and an experience to add to my (and Jason's) SCV (Sexual Curriculum Vitae). Mmmm, on second thoughts perhaps that should be renamed to GIHFFFFAF (Girls I Have Fucked for Fun, Friendship and Fame) CV.

For the next few days, Jason was like a dog on heat. I was up and down so many times that it was like a continuous traffic light sequence. Turn green and I was up, red I was down and amber left me uncertain of which way I was heading. The Balls complained about getting no sleep and the guys up at The Sperm Factory were busting for some relief time. But that wasn't to be. Jason had taken Kyle's advice very seriously, about needing to be horny enough to last an entire day of filming, so that meant no sex - and no whacking off - for the three days before.

So, there I was doing all this pumping to erection, then pulling the pressure plug, then trying to get a bit of downtime for myself before the next bout. It was continuous. Every time he thought of Trixie, up I went. And that was OFTEN! It was times like that where "Best Friends" can have a serious parting of the ways with their owners who under-estimate the effort in pumping and releasing all that blood. Even when I grabbed some shut-eye during his sleeping, there were several overnight woody's where I had to go through the motions even though he wasn't at all conscious of my efforts. I restrained myself in messaging him so that we didn't end up with an involuntary wet dream. If that had happened, he would have been furious at me.

The Wednesday night, 3am woody was the hardest to control. The Cum Busters control room up at The Sperm Factory wanted all systems "go" as they were by then in crisis with an over-production schedule looming. They were still working on the "horny-twenty-seven-year-old-24/7 production schedule" which allowed for no downtime whatsoever. Supplies just had to be maintained and that of course, meant that yesterday's production had to be released to a waiting world on a continuous supply basis. With Jason abstaining from his part of the bargain, it was crisis time internally - big time!

"Just a small release over the spillway" they tweeted down to The Balls. "P-L-E-A-S-E. We simply can't hold back the volume much longer...."

Such was their anguished cry that The Balls sent on the urgent message to me to get cracking on opening up the chute. The sheer intensity of the message woke me from a deep slumber and in my hazy state I accidentally pressed the ancillary Erection Muscle.

WHOAHHHHHH!!!!!! I had erected at quite the wrong time, hence a message soon filtered down from a now semi-conscious Boss asking "what the fuck is going on down there. I've got to be up and out of bed in three hours, now let me go back to sleep...."

Now I was in a dilemma - erect and no approval or physical encouragement to shoot a load - and with the upstairs banging away with a stream of ever-more-urgent "gotta dump some overage" messages it was a situation I really hadn't faced often in the past. Even that time confined to the hospital we managed a wank or three to keep the internal levels naturally turning over, and on the plane on the long flight to Europe, the toilets allowed enough privacy to shoot a cum-load at thirty-five thousand feet. No, this was new. I had to play for time so that Jason could feel all the pressures of a constrained cum-load during his impending fluffing day and fulfill his obligations on set.

Quickly I pulled the plug on the Erection Muscle and just like an airbed crumpling back to its limp state, so I deflated in the same direction. That meant those Nerve-End Boys became less intense in their stimulation activities and finally, they went back to sleep. Jason would now only feel a nothingness so he too, was soon back asleep. I put a block on my message center which effectively stopped messages from The Balls and The Sperm Factory, at least for a few hours. We all knew it was going to be a big day ahead and that we all had to effectively work together to give Jason the co-ordinated horniness that he required. With an additional three hour's rest, we were ready and prepared for it.

"Bring on Trixie - we backroom boys are ready!"

The set was indeed a glorious mansion located up in the heavily vegetated hills area. Lots of entertaining areas, a pool, beds (both inside and out), several people setting up camera, sound and lighting equipment and several very scantily-clad women obviously wearing nothing underneath their near see-through clothing.

"This is where you can change - and through there is make-up" Jason was instructed. "But right now meet the guys who you will be working for - Charley - or as you would know him, "Hung Ten" - and Brad and Matthew. Today's shoot is all about an orgy, so we need these guys up and hard when I say "two minutes". Right!"

"Sure, sir. I'll do my best."

"Son, it might be your first day as a fluffer to the stars, but your best is not why you're here. Kyle said that you could keep a boner for hours and that you've sucked dick on occasion. Do that to keep my boys up and ready for action, and you and I will get along famously."

Jason was by then a little confused as to his role - why would virile hetero guys want another naked straight guy to excite them? Wouldn't they need a slinky female?

"And in case you're wondering, Amy over there will also help you look after the mixed needs. Not all the guys are straight you know and neither are some of the women. Between the two of you, I'm sure all needs will be catered for. Now strip off, and show me your wares...."

"Dick-sucking?" responded Jason under his breath. Jason obviously hadn't factored into his thinking what the role of fluffer would actually entail. He and I had watched many hours of porn together, his eyes on the screen, his hand pumping me gently. What hadn't crossed his mind was actually how they filmed the movie - not in one long take or with multiple cameras as you might imagine, but in short chunks that allowed the single cameraman to move to a new position for a close-up or whatever. That meant the actors had many breaks before resuming their last position with a new camera angle. And with each break, erections inevitably wilted. Therefore, to bring the male actors back to whatever state of erection they were in when the camera stopped rolling was the role of the fluffer. That is, to fluff their erections so that the audience viewing the final video would not notice any difference following the edit.

The fluffer needed to be handsome, well hung, friendly, horny, sexually experienced and be able to turn-on jaded male porn actors (and some female ones) when all the actors really wanted to do was get paid and get out of there. He needed to always act as if he was the subject of their desires and that if they wanted to, they could fuck with him for real, right there and then.

Amy was already naked when we walked across to meet

her. A big welcoming smile when she saw me indicated that she was going to enjoy the day with this new handsome stud and his wouldn't-be-out-of-place-on-a-pornshoot appendage. I gave my head a little flick-dance of happiness in response.

"They shot one of the cum scenes yesterday" she responded as if we were experienced fluffers who knew the drill. "So today will be relatively easy. The gay boys will really like you, I can tell. The fresh farm-boy look always goes down a treat."

Hung, Brad, and Matthew headed for the set near the pool where the two big beds were pushed together.

"Well, hello big boy," said Brad as his hand stroked a warm welcome to me. "You're such a handsome one aren't you."

Well I know I am, I quietly thought to myself. A warm male hand other than Jason's was a somewhat rare occurrence for me, but being the slut that I am, I'll wallow in appreciation that comes from anyone. Mind you, like Jason, I was very interested in Miss Amy, all naked, all feminine, all very shaved and tempting. Perhaps we could turn-on the cast by letting them watch Amy and me turn-on to one another.

"I'll second that," said Amy, also giving me a stroking.

Desired by everyone!!!! OOOhhhhh I do so love being the center of attention. Now, where is that Trixie woman Jason is so infatuated with?

When everyone else was on set, a strong aroma of over-applied scent wafted past us as Trixie arrived, totally naked, ready for her moments before the camera.

This was the beginning of the orgy sequence, so it was all getting-to-know-you, setting-the-scene, type action. Therefore, flaccid dicks and smooth naked shaved pussy were all that was required. Our role could wait until mid-morning so Jason and I and Miss Amy just stood back and watched.

No, I'm not in the least embarrassed to say that I went straight to erection mode as soon as the six of them on that bed started the sensual kissing, the eating out and the dick-sucking. I quite simply couldn't take my eye off of it. I was looking both upwards and outwards and I could see Jason was similarly transfixed, whereas Amy seemed bored witless. She'd seen it all so many times before. To her, this was just a job. To Jason, it was Porn Central, Orgy World and Clit Kringle all rolled into one fabulous fantasy.

After the morning food break, we heard the command "Two minutes. Two minutes, ladies and gentlemen."

That was our cue. The three leading actors, all limp from drinking protein shakes and cola and phoning their partners to organize domestic arrangements, made their way to us.

"Suck my dick, bitch" was the command to Amy, who immediately fell to her knees to oblige the hunky co-star.

Brad watched that scene for a moment and began to slightly enlarge. I was eye-to-eye with his Best Friend and was suitably impressed. Suddenly I was thrust down between his knees as Jason, now also on his knees, began to suck his dick. Fuck, what brought that on so quickly I thought? But as I looked up I could see a firm hand behind Jason's head holding him in position so that Brad could pump into that orifice just enough to bring him to total hardness. In a few seconds, he was gone, back on set and ready to perform. Amy had worked her own miracle on Matthew and as I had noticed out of the corner of my eye, Mr. Hung had fluffed himself up just by watching the show in front of him. The erotica score so far: one gay, two straight or possibly bi. They were soon back on set and ready to continue.

FUCK! It all suddenly went pitch black. Amy had made her own move and I was deep throating her as enthusiastically as I've ever done it to anyone. I could hear the muffled "Quiet, please. Action..." from the pool patio area but the instructions from up above made no concession to that.

"Deeper! Deeper! Fuck, I so need to shoot a load, oh fuck yeah. Don't hold back buddy, give it to her. Give it to her.... yeah, yeah... NOWWWWWWWWWW."

Jason tried to muffle it, but with a huge relief-sounding "F-A-A-A-R-K" flowing from his mouth, he couldn't help himself.

I spewed a bucket load. I couldn't hold back. Those Cum Busters in the flood-control room finally got their way. It wasn't just a small spillway release - it was a torrent. The Balls had no control over its volume so all they could say was "straight through here boys. No stopping, no barriers!"

And what could I do when faced with the torrent but open the floodgates. I was amazed at how quickly my own head was swimming in the abundant juices when even the obviously very experienced and talented Amy couldn't swallow enough to empty her mouth.

The cry "CUT" could be heard across the entire pool,

bed and house area.

And then, huge applause and lots of whoops and whistles.

As it was explained later, this was like an initiation into the world of porn. Just about every male newcomer to a porn set, whether fluffer or not, seems to be immediately turned-on by all the open eroticism, and few ever miss the chance to masturbate or otherwise get off while watching the filming. When it's noticed by the cast or crew, that rite-of-passage moment is acknowledged. It also makes the fluffer's job even more desirable later in the shoot as the actors by then know that it's all about everyone on the set loving sex, sharing sex and having the camaraderie of being with like-minded work colleagues.

Towards the end of the lunch break, the lounge area where Amy and Jason were fluffing could have been filmed for a second movie. At various times, I was being sucked by one of the girls - and then by one of the boys. Jason was eating pussy and sucking breasts, Amy was having a dick massage between her large breasts, two of the female stars were kissing in a same-sex embrace, Trixie sat on me to try me out for size and pleasure, all the while the rather distressed director was trying to get his two-minute call heeded to and his filming schedule back on track.

Jason and I loved all the attention, and the earlier sexplosion episode had worked wonders for our popularity. I had no difficulty in staying erect nor worrying about whose mouth was doing what. Brief that it was when Trixie sat on me for a "size fitting" as she called it, I was ecstatic. For a few moments, she was the center of my universe. I was touching fame from the inside out. My head was in touch with the very intimacy of her femininity. She was very famous and greatly adored by her huge male fan base - and now a little bit of that fame had rubbed off on me along with the lube. Let the afternoon roll on as however, it may....

By late afternoon there were only a couple of close-ups or "money shots" to be filmed. One had already been done yesterday as Amy had previously told us - that was with the superstar, Hung - but today two more were required. With the first new cum shot from Brad successfully captured for posterity, the cast, including Matthew and some of the crew, began heading off, oblivious to the fact that there was still a final "money shot" to be captured.

When it was discovered that Matthew had gone, the director realized that he needed a substitute dick in order to capture that all important final climax shot.

The director himself had performed a climax shot many times before in order to finish his film, but that day he knew he'd get much better spillage from having a younger more virile man do the shot.

"Want to earn an extra two hundred?" he said to Jason. "Then get yourself and that great dick of yours over here right away."

Amy had seen this sort of fakery many times before so she knew that even the fluffer might need a bit of a hand to earn his two hundred.

"Keep your hand over the pubes, for Matty is clean-shaven so we have to disguise...." said the director.

Amy went down on me again and used her lips and

tongue to experienced perfection. After removing herself from my now internally pulsing shaft I positively glistened in the late afternoon sun as her saliva dripped from my head and along the shaft. With a hand movement or two, I was away, shooting a spiral of creamy rope high into the air, quickly followed by additional jets of juicy jizz to complete the required sticky scenario. The boys upstairs in The Sperm Factory had saved and indeed, had topped up the morning losses so that my ten seconds of fame (actually twenty-five when the slow motion is edited in) would be captured in all its creamy white glory for millions of tossers the world over to admire. They would, of course, think that it was Matt shooting his load.

But my friends, you and I can share the secret that I am indeed a porn star, even though I am an uncredited name. And every time Jason and I watch Bed-Delicious Bombshells we both have silent, gratifying smiles knowing that in bedrooms, sex cinemas and back rooms of offices we are helping bring relief to another horny man or woman through our magnificent unheralded eruption. How many other penises do you know that can be masturbated to climax while watching themselves on screen in a professional porn production? Jason loves it so much it's his most watched video on his smart-phone.

Now, let me think - how can I get a belated royalty payment and on-screen credit from that now porn superstar, Matty – or as he's better known, Matt Missile: The Dick of Death!

After all, it's not called a "money shot" for nothing, is it?

PETER BENN

POSTSCRIPT

My Life as a Penis

A pickle, a cucumber, and a penis were talking about life.

The cucumber said when I get big and hard they chop me up and toss me in a salad.

The pickle said when I get big and hard they chop me up and drown me in vinegar.

The penis said when I get big and hard they put a plastic bag over my head, put me in a dark damp cave and then bang my head against the walls until I throw up!

Anonymous

I couldn't have said it better.

I know my place in Jason's life and as you've now read, I truly love my work.

Hopefully, very soon, I'll be able to bring my pleasure to you, too!

PETER BENN

If you enjoyed this read

then tell a friend,

buy them a copy,

or shout about it on social media.

And if you have a moment, a brief review on any book website would be greatly appreciated.

Independent authors like myself just love having their works talked about.

By doing this you'll be helping many more enjoyable books to get written and published.

Thanks!

PETER BENN

Other Books by Peter Benn

TALES FROM THE FUR SIDE: Purrfectly Adorable Cat Stories (e-book and paperback)
A collection of entertaining tall tales, and (possibly) true, from the secret lives of cats - as told by the cats themselves! Mischief. Mayhem. History. Heroism. Revenge and Reflection - this is life as lived on the fur-side, beyond the prying eyes of humans – where wisdom, adventure, and love mix abundantly with mystery, murder and exotic locations. An ideal gift for anyone who is loved by a cat.

"Oh what a fun little read this was." Amazon Review

VERSATILE HUSBAND, The (e-book and paperback)
Answers all the questions a married man might ask about same-sex attraction.

"A straightforward practical guide for men in heterosexual relationships who'd like to explore sex with other men. Frank, honest and understanding." Kirkus Reviews

Also, visit Peter's informative blog at
http://theversatilehusband.blogspot.com.au

EVERY DAY IS YOUR BEST DAY (e-book and paperback)
When life looks all doom and gloom, change it – easily, today. We can't change the bigger picture, but we can change ourselves by embracing aspects of our daily living that will give us comfort, happiness, abundance, optimism and a strong base for individual growth. Written with wisdom and using real-life experiences, this New Age approach to inner contentment is exactly what is needed during this time of change and uncertainty.

"This book was truly inspirational." GoodReads

CRUISE EXCURSIONS: Plan Your Best Ever European or Baltic Cruise (e-book)
aka **CRUISE EXCURSIONS: 25 of the Best European Cruise Ship and Baltic Cruise Ship Shore Trips** (paperback)
Get the immediate flavor of 25 ports and cities with this invaluable quick-look thumbnail planning guide based on the author's actual shore trip experiences. Includes an invaluable checklist of what to take with you to make your shore excursion happy and stress-free.

"This is an extremely practical book." Amazon Review

www.peterbenn.com

Also from Argosy Media

THE BOOK LOVERS (e-book) by Bradley Fox
Set a decade ago in vibrant London, Scotland, the Riviera and aboard an all-male gay Mediterranean cruise, this captivating M/M romance will delight the reader who believes that true love conquers all and that whatever the odds, true hearts are destined to find one other.
"Very sweet story with a satisfactory happy ending. Great potential in this author, hoping to see more adventurous efforts and edgy storylines." Amazon Review

PETER BENN

www.ingramcontent.com/pod-product-compliance
Lightning Source LLC
Chambersburg PA
CBHW070538010526
44118CB00012B/1169